THE STORY OF
TULLANS COUNTRY HOLIDAY PARK

The Seasons of My Life

DIANA MCCLELLAND

'The boundary lines have fallen for me in pleasant places; surely I have a delightful inheritance.' Psalm 16:6

Dedication

To my loving husband, gone to be with the Lord.

29 May 1938 – 21 October 2020

THE SEASONS OF MY LIFE

Published by

Maurice Wylie Media
Your Inspirational & Christian Book Publisher

For more information visit
www.MauriceWylieMedia.com

Testimonials

Memories of Tullans Throughout the Years

From 1992, four close-knit families from County Armagh — the Alderdice, Davison, Fulton and Hyde — began their Tullans adventure with touring caravans. It all began with a warm welcome from Diana during our first stay, and from that moment, we never considered staying anywhere else. Over the years, we've created cherished memories that continue to bring us joy.

Happy moments abound, from egg decorating at Easter, with excited children hoping to win the prize of a big Easter egg, to lamb feeding and charity events throughout the year. End-of-season parties. Halloween fireworks, games of tug of war, and wellie-boot throwing always culminated in a delightful barbecue or stew night, complete with home-made apple tarts — utterly delicious! We even celebrated the 2012 Queen's Diamond Jubilee in grand style, with Diana and Norman dressed as Queen Elizabeth and Prince Philip. And then who could forget the unforgettable Tullans Fest in 2017.

I have lovely memories of going to Diana's kitchen to pay at the end of every stay and settle the bill, with a good chat of course, and surrounded by the delicious aroma of potatoes in the pot or apple tarts in the oven.

We all eventually grew out of our touring caravans and the four families bought statics on pitches side by side to accommodate our growing families with twelve children, and then their husbands, wives, boyfriends, girlfriends, twenty-three grandchildren and still counting. All of us love staying at Tullans — a *'Home away from Home.'*

Gale

We purchased our first touring van in 1989, and being novices, we joined the Christian Caravanners (CCCF) for guidance on various aspects like gas, awnings, reversing, etc. They introduced us to several sites, among which Tullans stood out immediately as a favourite. We felt it was safe for seven-year-old daughter. The long lane from the road and excellent safety signage around the site allowed us to relax while Ruth disappeared to make the most of the opportunities for fun and friendship with the other young folk on the site. The well-equipped play park and games room for wet days became her world and she made a range of friendships that she still enjoys today. Once she headed to the park, she was gone for the morning, although from time to time she and her friends passed the van on one of their manhunts or in search of some hidden treasure. In turn, Ruth's daughter, Caitlyn, and sons, Adam, and Josh, took the same opportunities to make friends and enjoy outdoor fun with the Tullans gang.

On visits when none of her friends were about, our only child Ruth developed another strategy to enjoy her time on site. She could be seen heading for a newly - arrived van and knocking on the door to see if they had any dogs that needed walking. We were never surprised to see her roaming the site with a dog in one hand and a poo bag in the other. One of her favourite canine adoptees was a dog called Teena, and five years later, when she finally persuaded us to get a dog, it too had to be called Teena.

One of the unique features of Tullans for 'townies' was the fact that it was a working farm. Ruth loved all the animals but really enjoyed lambing season. She disappeared to the barns and on one occasion took us to see her cuddle the newborns. From time to time, she even helped Diana serve breakfasts in the B&B site. It was hardly surprising that there was never any problem persuading Ruth to join us on a trip to Tullans.

2008 was the start of a new era for us in our Tullans relationship: when a faulty neck disc and five hours of neurosurgery left me with instructions to avoid dragging a ton of caravan and awning equipment about. Fortunately, Tullans had a solution in the form of a six-berth Cosalt Albany Static caravan. This allowed us to get there faster, store more bikes and surfboards, enjoy barbecues and, most importantly, it threw us together with families in adjacent statics. As a result, we made great friendships with a lovely family from Dundonald and a fun-loving single lady from the *Maiden City*.

Caravanning over the last thirty-four years would not have been the same for us without Tullans and we hope the next generation of '*Turtles*' will continue to enjoy this little gem of a site and the great family who run it.

Denise & Brian Turtle

Almost three decades ago, Diana and Norman entered our lives and changed them forever.

On a whim, we bought a battered, run-down tourer van, and after a lick of paint and a bit of polish, we planned our adventure to tour the length and breadth of Ireland, Scotland, Wales and England. After that it was wherever the wind took us in Europe.

As complete novice caravan greenhorns, our parents suggested a trial weekend away with the caravan somewhere on the north coast. As retirees, they set off to find caravan sites around the Portrush triangle that we might try. There was no internet back then!

They returned absolutely gushing about *"This beautiful site near Coleraine owned by the loveliest lady called Diana."* She had talked to them for ages and introduced her husband Norman and assured them that we would be most welcome.

We set off one Friday evening for our trial weekend before we began our great travel adventure, and the most perfect thing happened - we never left Tullans! And we never toured or visited another site!

It's a joy and a privilege, and a blessing to be a part of the McClelland family at Tullans to this very day. The piece of heaven that is Tullans is down to the fact that Diana and Norman opened their arms and welcomed every stranger to their home.

Joan & Brian Chambers

Contents

Foreword 1

The welcome at Tullans is, like Diana's wonderful culinary skills, exceptionally good for the soul. Any length of time spent there is well seasoned with exceptional kindness, good humour, wisdom and love. For over 50 years that has largely been down to Norman and Diana. It doesn't matter who you are, or where you have come from, they have always been invariably generous in sharing their lives with friends and strangers alike.

My wife Pat and I have always enjoyed time with them. In the 1980's when I frequently called at the farm, I tried to engineer the timing of my visits with Norman's midmorning *'elevenses'* – a feast for all the senses. As I reminisce on the aroma and flavours of Diana's freshly baked breads, the hilarious tales of farming adventures from Norman and, in the summer, the children eager to play and share their latest escapades, I am reminded that those were great days indeed.

I know you will enjoy reading Diana's story. She is a strong and determined woman, full of enterprise - a born leader that many look up to, in her wider family, in the church and in the community. She is a deeply caring woman. Many have been blessed by her generous kindness and found a true counsellor and friend when it was most needed. God, by His grace, through adversity and joy, has forged a woman of deep Christian faith and character.

I hope you will benefit from reading her story as Diana's life has been far from solitary, as she joyfully tells us in this volume. But it has left an immense impact for good on so many others. It is my prayer that her story, as recorded here, has a similar effect on the reader.

The seasons of Diana's life have all been *'well-seasoned'* with the grace, mercy and peace of God. This volume is a further illustration of her desire to bless others with the goodness of the Lord. I hope as you taste and see, you will know that the Lord is good.

Rev Dr Graham Connor B Sc.

Retired after serving in Ballyrashane, Bloomfield and 2nd Saintfield Presbyterian Churches.

Foreword 2

I have never forgotten the Diana I met in the early days of her business aspirations: she was quiet and a little lacking in confidence, mainly due to something unkind that a teacher had said to her many years before, words that had not inspired self-confidence. Diana had enrolled on our Women in Business course to explore the tentative idea of starting a caravan site on her family farm but was still 'working on her husband' in the hope that he would believe in her venture enough to risk giving up a field.

In what seemed like no time at all, I bumped into a friend who had been to stay at Tullans Farm caravan site and thought it was fantastic. "She's only gone and done it!" I thought to myself. I was so happy to hear that Diana's venture was up and running and hoped that she was proud of her achievement and could begin to put those unkind words from her past to rest.

Some years later, when I learned that Diana had won the Business Woman of the Year award, I was chuffed to bits for her and so proud that she had gone from strength to strength in her business and that this had been recognised.

When I ran into Diana again a few years ago, I found her to be incredibly humble about the thriving business that she has created in our local economy, but with a quiet assurance that now seemed deeply rooted within herself.

There may be many different versions of entrepreneurial success but Diana has shown that a willingness to put in the hard work, face the obstacles and persevere towards your dream can be enormously rewarding. I'm very glad her husband gave her that first field! Diana now has quite a legacy to pass on to the next generation and should be proud of all she has accomplished.

Joy Wisener

Business Development Officer for Coleraine Enterprise Agency, 1990-2002. (now Enterprise Causeway.)

Chapter 1

Location, Location, Location

The town of Coleraine is situated five miles from where the long-travelled waters of the river reach the Atlantic Ocean at Barmouth. The Bann River, the largest in Northern Ireland, falls into two distinct parts. The Upper Bann rises in the Mourne Mountains and flows north-west into Lough Neagh. The Lower Bann flows northward through Lough Beg and carries the waters of Lough Neagh to the sea below Coleraine. The total length is 80 miles (129 km). The lower river occupies a peaty depression in the basalt plateaus of Ballymena, Ballymoney, Coleraine and Magherafelt districts. Upstream the waterpower from the river played an important part in the industrialization of the linen industry. The river also has valuable salmon and eel fisheries which are the most important economic features of the river, plus there is the valley at the prehistoric site at Mountsandel.

Prehistoric remains of the Mesolithic and Neolithic period have been found there and it is now recognised as the earliest known settlement in Ireland. Archaeology digs on Mountsandel Fort have uncovered remains of the first human arrivals in Ireland, dating back to 7600 and 7900 BC. Flint tools were found here, indicating that Stone Age hunters camped here to fish salmon in the natural weir. The earthen fort is thought to date back to Norman times. The name Coleraine derives from the Irish name, *'Cuil Rathain,'* meaning Ferny Corner, which also refers to the patch of ground reputed to be the site of the Church of St Patrick. This land in the town centre was presented to

St Patrick when he was expounding the argument that the history of Ireland and its people was a product of the mingling, not always peacefully or purposefully, of cultures far beyond its shores. Successive waves of settlement and visitations in the last 1,500 years, involving Celts, Vikings, Normans, and the English, as well as Highland and Lowland Scots, have been influenced by the strategic significance of its position. Indeed, the historical and geographical importance of the coastline between Coleraine and Ballycastle are tellingly illustrated by the fate of those Spanish Armada ships, which were blown off course while fleeing from their defeat by Sir Francis Drake in the English Channel in 1588, foundering on the spectacular and stormy North Antrim coast. Artefacts were retrieved some fifty years ago.

In the early seventeenth century the Plantation of Ulster was the last of the four provinces of Ireland to be planted by the Crown, and was centred on several planned towns, of which Coleraine was a fine example. More than that, it was central to the settlement of the new County Londonderry, formerly named the County of Coleraine, by a group of twelve London livery companies who established a holding company called the Irish Society. Our four children attended The Irish Society's primary school in Coleraine.

Coleraine was incorporated by Royal Charter in 1613, and from then began to assume its role as a town and port serving the counties of Londonderry and Antrim. The charter recognised Coleraine's pre-eminence as a seaport and its economic activity enabled it to become, by the 1680s, the third largest port in Ulster, behind Derry and Armagh, but interestingly far ahead of Belfast.

In the eighteenth century, ships from the ports of Coleraine and Portrush added their passengers to the significant stream of emigrants who found their way from Ulster to colonial North America. The latter part of the nineteenth century saw the introduction of the manufacturing of garments, agricultural implements and milk-processing factories, adding to its post-war prosperity. One of the town's characteristics was its good reputation for educational provision. 1968 saw the arrival of the New University of Ulster, Northern Ireland's second university which acknowledged that tradition. On its tenth anniversary, the vice chancellor said, *"Our long-term objective [...] is to play our part in providing for Northern Ireland an institution which will be new not only in its structure but in its concept of service. Being new is in some ways being orthodox, but it does not mean being of second quality [...] in the ultimate analysis the success of the university will depend not only on the students who come to it because it happens to have places available but on the quality of staff and students who are attracted to it because of its reputation as a teaching institution and in research."* [1]

On reflection, over fifty years, and despite the Troubles, economic crises and many other obstacles, Ulster University at Coleraine has survived to become a very successful seat of learning and is still thriving today. It is home to over 30,000 students and welcomes international students from more than seventy countries.

---

[1] Excerpt from The New University of Ulster anniversary brochure 1978.

Chapter 2

Diana Rosemary - That's Me!

I t was Tuesday May 28, 1946, when I opened my eyes to the world in the Mary Ranken Maternity Hospital on Castlerock Road, Coleraine. Apparently, I was a contented baby with brown hair. I was also a good feeder (some things never change). This was a home from home and Mum and I were discharged on the ninth day. The weekly rate was £4.15 shillings for a private room plus 15 shillings for the operating theatre. That would be £4.75 in 2023.

The local doctors bought the Mary Ranken building after fund-raising efforts, and in 1891, the first patient was admitted to the first cottage hospital in Coleraine. It was then sold to Dr Ranken Lyle from Newcastle-upon-Tyne who had relatives in Aghadowey, who in turn handed it over to a trust in 1929, hence Mary Ranken. The area is now the site of Clanmil Housing Association which accommodates independent living for the elderly, and is called Hezlet Court, named after Vice Admiral Sir Arthur Richard Hezlet, KBE, CB, DSO, and Bar, DSC, Legion of Merit (USA) (1914–2007). He was a decorated Royal Navy submariner and at thirty-six was the youngest to be promoted to captain. At forty-six he was the youngest admiral. He was born in Pretoria, South Africa where his father was serving and was educated at the Royal Naval College, Dartmouth. He, his wife and two daughters lived at Bovagh House in Aghadowey. Sir Arthur died in 2007, aged ninety-three.

I was named Diana Rosemary, and was known as Rosemary for a week, before my parents reverted to Diana at the registration of my birth. My mum was baptised Diana, although Dad called her Anna all her married life. My great aunt was Diana, so I suppose it was an automatic choice in the end. As I grew older, for some unknown reason, Dad had a habit of calling me Dag, especially if he was in good form. *"Hi Dag, come over here,"* was often heard around the house. Dag Hammarskjold was a Swedish diplomat who served as the second secretary general of the United Nations from April 1953, until his death in a plane crash in September 1961. I always regret not asking my dad why he associated me with that name.

I was born into a family of four, with two elder and two younger brothers. My mum must have been very fit as she told me she cycled six miles to her parents' house two days before I was born. There were no Joe Wicks or personal trainers in those days, just good fresh air and natural exercise. My mum came from a farm at Ballynacannon near Macosquin and had two sisters and a brother.

Dad was born in Caheny near Moneydig and had three elder sisters. His eldest sister was a missionary in Brazil and is buried in Rio de Janeiro. His dad died when he was a teenager, and he was subsequently left with a burden of debt on the farm. There was a serious economic downturn in farming in the late 1920s. He recalled farmers dumping potatoes behind the hedges because there was no market for them - and many other farm products. This was not a time to travel, but Dad did just that on 24 August 1928, when he headed across the world to the land of opportunity at the age of twenty. *RMS Transylvania* set sail from Glasgow and docked at Londonderry, then dropped anchor in Moville, where Dad boarded the ship enroute to New York. Always an early bird, Thomas Hogg, my dad was number one on the passenger list. According to the *RMS Transylvania* entry on Wikipedia, the following is noted about the ship my dad sailed on: *'RMS Transylvania was launched in March 1925, for the Anchor Line and was a sister ship to the SS Californian and RMS Caledonia. She was converted into an*

armed merchant cruiser, pennant F56 during World War II. On August
10, 1940, HMS Transylvania was torpedoed and sunk by the German
U-boat U 56' [2].

The autumn of 1929 saw the Wall Street Crash. The Great Depression
sent waves of economic distress to most countries across the world
and lasted until 1939. However, Dad secured a well-paid job on the
underground railway in New York and stayed there for seven years.
During that period, he frequently sent home money to help clear
the farm debt, but never returned home during that time himself.
However, in due course, the urge to return to his homeland tugged at his
heartstrings and he set his sights again upon Ireland. Disappointingly,
on his arrival he was met with sad news - the farm had been sold to
a neighbour; the dwelling house was all that remained. Even sadder
was the fact that the money he sent home was evidently insufficient
to reduce the debt, so the sale of the farm was inevitable. Being the
resilient man that he always was, and having enough reserves, he
bought the Knockaduff farm and lived there on his own for three
years. Apparently, this young *'American'* cut a dash at the dances with
his flashy US tailored suits and clean-cut hairstyle. My mum had
been dating someone else when Dad came on the scene and she fell
for him hook, line and sinker. Dad always had a glint in his eyes,
so I could understand how she was attracted to him. They married
on the 19th of February 1941, in Ringsend Presbyterian Church
and a honeymoon baby boy arrived in November the same year. I
think Dad thought he was in the Promised Land when he occupied
Knockaduff. In later years it became site of historical interest too. A
local newspaper describes the historical importance of this area in the
following extract:

'The Bronze Age bones were found in the summer of 1937. Mr Tom
Smith of Knockaduff, in the Parish of Aghadowey, was digging in gravel
pit, when portions of two urns were unearthed. These had been deposited
about eighteen inches below the surface on a site which was a gravel dump
deposited by the retreating Clyde Glazier and the associated outwash in a

[2] https://en.wikipedia.org/wiki/RMS_Transylvania_(1925)

south-easterly direction to the Bann. The tiny stream, which we have now is but the remnants of mighty rivers which vented the waters of the melted ice. The River Bann was once as big as the Mississippi, and the Macosquin as big as the Bann. The fragments of the urns have been examined by experts and pronounced to have been two pots, about fifteen inches in height and twelve inches in diameter. The decoration consists of a band of incised lines arranged to form a chevron pattern on the outside of the vessel near the rim, in one case, and in the other, a decoration of a band of rings both inside and outside. A piece of bronze found with the pots seems to be a piece of waste from the inside of a crucible. The date of the vessels is probably late Bronze Age i.e., 2,500 years ago. Of extreme interest, are the bones found with the urns. The bone fragments are the thoroughly calcined remains of an adult human incineration, and include the socket for a thigh bone, and also leg bones of the right side. The subject was probably the male species. The bones show no sign of disease. By the size of the upper end of the femur, the large angle of femoral neck, and the density of the bone cortex, it is likely that the bones are that of a tall, round-headed, mid-age, Bronze Age incomer rather than a short, long-headed indigenous inhabitant. Knockaduff, which is beautifully situated on the Macosquin river, has a carious little tumulus (if the townland is pronounced Knockadoo), it means the "hill of the tumulus" called "The Tooosie", a word which baffles the Gaelic experts, but in all likelihood refers to a chieftain buried there ("Taisei" — a chieftain). There is a townland of Lissan, near Cookstown and it has a rath.

That so much can be told from these artifacts, teaches us the lesson that all relics of the past be carefully and respectfully treasured, for only by these things can we reconstruct our history and learn of the pit from which we were dug and the rock from which we were hewn'.[3]

One Sunday afternoon, my brothers, along with some friends, made a five-a-side football team and headed over to the 'moor' field, it being the farthest field and out of sight. Dad got wind of it and while the game was in full flow, an angry *'referee'* went on to the pitch and slashed the football with his penknife. *"That'll finish the game today,*

---

[3] The Northern Constitution, January 1937

boys," he said. Dad was not usually bad tempered, but if you crossed the line, he put on his boss's hat.

His soft nature was very evident when the two agricultural horses were made redundant and Dad took delivery of his first, wee-grey *Fergie* tractor on the farm. When the horses were loaded on to the transport lorry, he took me by the hand, and we went upstairs and watched out the window as the lorry weaved its way down the Knockaduff Road and disappeared towards Kilrea to an unknown destination. My dad's tears flowed, and I think mine did too.

The plantation across the road, which was also the farm boundary, was the first port of call in the spring for our young family. It was an amazing wonderland, with its birch, hazel and beech trees. In the middle there was an old, gnarled arched tree, hard to climb, which we called *'the devil's elbow.'* It produced a prolific crop of juicy apples each year. My brothers and I arrived there every Easter, armed with a tin can, firewood, methylated spirits and the proverbial eggs. The tin, filled with water and gorse blossom we'd plucked, was infused before the eggs were gently submerged into the yellow liquid and boiled until they were as hard as bricks. We then proceeded to the *'swing brae'* to roll the eggs. The rolling of the eggs signified the rolling away of the stone from Jesus's tomb.

Although surrounded by boys, I was well chaperoned by my brothers, 'and I never experienced any trouble or improper attention from the boys.' Our neighbours, the McQuiggs, Gillespies, and Cunninghams were all very respectful of my gender.

One sunny Sunday afternoon, two of my brothers, a few neighbours and I, set off in an overloaded car destined for Portrush. The harbour was our first choice where a rowing boat was duly hired, and we set off for the Skerries - with no lifejackets and no knowledge of the tides. Halfway across, the *'skipper'* decided to change course and we headed back to the safety of the harbour. On returning home, our parents were never informed of our seafaring escapade in the Atlantic Ocean. Although Dad was a great advocate of Sunday observance and tried his best to instil it into his children, he didn't always succeed.

Life in the early fifties was less complicated than it is today, and school days were no different. In 1951 I started Culcrow Primary School, which was only a mile away from home. Although I was a strong girl in many ways, I was extremely shy and craved encouragement, but I was seldom given any at school. The head teacher had peculiar traits and he didn't ooze with encouragement. I had long strawberry-blonde hair which I sometimes wore in plaits. I was of medium build and had a fierce appetite that made me as heavy as lead when I was a child. Much of my work and effort went unnoticed. When I was in the senior class the headteacher mockingly called me *Lightning* because I was so slow. When I recognised some of his traits, I soon realised this man had a disliking towards me and I felt demoralised, especially in front of the other pupils, and it gave me an inferiority complex that stuck with me for many years. His manner was unknown to my parents and when they suggested I enter the eleven-plus exam, they were immediately told I wouldn't have a chance of passing. So, I can honestly say that I didn't fail as I didn't sit the exam. I never told my parents about the hurt I endured, although I can recall one or two other girls being similarly mistreated. The repercussions of this unfair treatment resurfaced occasionally throughout my life, but with God's help, I put it to rest. However, I do have some pleasant memories of Culcrow too. Every year the head teacher presented medals at Culcrow for complete attendance during the year. I received one each year and was the recipient of the Patricia Smythe Cup. Surprise! Surprise! This was for the *'most esteemed pupil'* in my final year. To subsidise school funds, the head teacher fattened pigs in a sty at the bottom of the school garden. The McGrath brothers, who were Coleraine butchers, delivered slops twice a week to feed the pigs ready for slaughter. As I was always early for school, Minnie Smith, who was the cook, had no assistant and I filled the breach. I rolled pastry for jam tarts, caramel squares with coconut, and I peeled potatoes and vegetables. Sadly, many years later, Minnie was fatally injured while crossing the road from the school. This was felt deeply by the whole community.

Incidentally, my dad slaughtered pigs on our farm and delivered the offal (liver, kidneys, trotters etc) around the less well-off neighbours. There were no Food Banks in those days.

When I was ten my mum took me to a Coleraine photographer to have my photograph taken before I had my hair cut for the first time. After the photo was taken, my hair was cut and put in a box for me to take home. I still have it. The following week my photograph appeared in the *Coleraine Chronicle*, the local weekly newspaper. This was published without permission and with my hair being measured. My crowning glory was supposed to be twenty-four inches long and the question submitted by the photographer was, *'Can anyone beat that length?'* Mum was furious and instantly realised it was a sales gimmick. In the six weeks that followed, photos of clients appeared and every time each one had an increased hair length. The last entry measured thirty-six and a half inches. All I can say is that he was a very successful, albeit shrewd businessman.

On one occasion when Mum trimmed my hair, my long tresses got entangled in a fly catcher. The fly catcher was a spiral of yellow sticky tape that hung from the kitchen ceiling. There was no escape when a fly flew into it - it meant instant death. Likewise, when my hair stuck to it. Mum came to my rescue, and cut off a small piece of my hair, which was the only way to free me.

Interestingly, flypaper was invented in 1861, by a German baker who hung a molasses-coated strip in his shop window. In the years that followed, arsenic was added. It is unlawful to use this substance today, although I remember my husband, before it became illegal, inserting it in a dead lamb to finish off its predators.

When I was eleven, I entered form 1A upper and remained in the top stream at Coleraine Girls' Secondary School. I held that position until

I left, after attaining high grades in all subjects, including prizes for projects, home economics and art at county level. After completing R.S.A. in English and Maths I planned to go Coleraine Technical College. However, a chance encounter with a prominent Coleraine businessman changed all my plans, as the saying goes: *'the best laid plans of mice and men...'* My parents were well-known customers of Tweedy Acheson and Co, The Diamond, Coleraine. One day, while I was in the shop with my parents, Mr Acheson approached me to ask what I was doing during the summer. In a discussion with my parents, an interview was set up and within two weeks I was in the retail business. My first position was in the haberdashery and household department. I was well trained in dealing with the general public and I really enjoyed the challenge. One of the many incidents, and there were many, I recall, was when a well-heeled couple came in to buy a blanket. I brought down most of the stock for inspection; I focused their attention on an excellent, but very expensive specimen. I emphasised that the *Sole Mio* with its exquisite silk binding was the best buy. I also told them that it was the blanket that Princess Margaret and Anthony Armstrong-Jones had used on their honeymoon in 1961, aboard the Royal Yacht *Britannia*. I'm positive that comment clinched the deal. The boss, Mr Acheson, was usually hovering around and liked to be present when a sale was executed. After the departure of the satisfied customers, he approached and asked me to come to the office. With fear and trepidation, I proceeded like a lamb to the slaughter. Ironically, he recognised my business acumen and offered me a pay rise, from £4 to £5 per week. He also opened a bank account for me and deposited a pound a week into it - what a difference in attitude to that of my headteacher at primary school. Mr Acheson subscribed £5 each to a friend and I who completed the 13 mile 'Triangle' (Coleraine-Portstewart-Portrush) charity walk during Coleraine Community Week in June 1963.

Part of my training in retail was to be discreet and keep confidentiality regarding customers. The longer I live, the I more I realise that those values, which were instilled in me so long ago, have been my yardstick in life and have equipped me with the ability to be trusted by everyone

I meet. Solomon in the Book of Proverbs writes strong and wise words concerning these virtues: 1) Whenever you are tempted to talk, do not yield. 2) Whenever you are discussing people do not repeat confidences. 3) However, if you are prone to disagree, do not slander.

I will share with you one example of that practice. By this stage I had received promotion to the ladies' fashions via the children's department. My boss asked me to go with him to buy stock in the fashion houses in London. Lack of confidence made me decline the offer. However, ladies' fashions were more appealing to me. A highly respected and affluent woman, well known for her fashion flair, had come to me to be fitted out. After I had dressed her with a fashionable, sophisticated and elegant outfit that included coat, hat, gloves, shoes and handbag, she left as a very satisfied customer. The next Sunday she met my mum as she entered church. She was well adorned from head to toe, and Mum felt obliged to admire her in her smart attire. *"Did Diana not tell you that she 'rigged' me out?"* the woman replied. Mum was pleased to say that I had never mentioned her name.

Aghadowey Church was not short of characters and Sammy Millar was one of them. He was small in stature with twinkling eyes and always witty in his speech. Sammy was accompanying Mum and Mrs T., a rather well-endowed and portly woman, up the church steps. *"It would lift you; it's a terribly stormy day,"* Mum said. *"Mrs Hogg, you'll be a good bit before Mrs T is lifting,"* Sammy replied.

John Arthur of Culdrum, the townland next to Knockaduff, was a farmer/handyman, who fixed anything from binders to threading pipes for plumbing jobs. He too was well characterized by his quick and inventive verbal humour, and always had a suitably witty answer for every occasion. He took his brother, James, who had been stung by a bee, to the local GP at Beechcroft, Aghadowey. It was late in the evening when he knocked the surgery door only to be confronted by a crabbit doctor. *"What are you doing here at this time of night?"* the doctor asked. *"I had to wait until the bee stung him,"* was the swift reply.

Chapter 3

Haymaking and Mice

I now more than ever realise what a privilege it was to grow up on a farm in a rural community and I will be forever grateful for the upbringing my loving parents gave me. There was a togetherness in the neighbourhood. If there was a need of any kind, there would be someone on your doorstep. The various farming seasons took place at regular intervals throughout the year.

The potato harvest was a busy time when Dad collected all the women from the neighbourhood to gather in the crop. They were very glad to augment the family income when basic wages for working families were very low. They were all good workers and Dad gave them a wee perk of turnips and cabbages along with their pay at the week's end. They really appreciated a mundane gift such as vegetables. A spinner was used to spin out each drill of potatoes and a pair of women took each side of the basket. A length was allotted to the pair and sometimes there was a dispute as to who got the biggest portion to gather. The full baskets were taken across the dug ground and emptied in a long pyramid-shaped pit which had to be straight. When it was a fair length another one was started. The pit was covered with straw and then rushes cut from a marshy meadow on the farm. A trench was dug alongside, and soil shovelled up to cover the entire pit and protect it from the winter frost. It was a good insulation exercise that protected them from the elements. When the potatoes were lifted in the winter, there were always a few holes where vermin had made their homes.

The tea break was always anticipated around 11 o'clock when Mum brought a basket laden with sodas, slims and pancakes, all baked daily, along with a big kettle of strong tea. Enamel mugs were the chosen receptacles. There were no hand sanitisers in those days. The working day was usually from 8 a.m. to 6 p.m. I well remember Mum helping in the fields. She wrapped my youngest brother, Ronnie, in a blanket and placed him in the horse's collar to sleep — a modern-day baby relax.

There were usually two or three threshing sessions every year. The exercise took place in the stack yard where the corn stacks were preserved over the winter. A circular base was made with thorn bushes and the stooks of corn were placed side by side with the stalks on the outside, while the seed heads were left in the centre. This made a nice circle about three metres in height, which then decreased in circumference with every row of sheaves until it came to an apex at the top. When it was completed the corn stack was covered with rushes and tied down diagonally across the thatch with grass ropes. In winter, when threshing day came, all the neighbours were commandeered to help. Some would fork the sheaves up to the man who fed them into the threshing mill, others bagged the seed or the chaff, which was used to bed and line the hen's nests, and more hands were needed to bale the straw, used to bed cattle and sheep. Every man had an assignment on that day. Some of the men tied their trouser legs closed with binder twine to prevent rats or mice escaping into them to seek shelter or a hiding place. Dad told me about a very brave man who squeezed a rat to death when it had made its way up his trouser leg. My worst memory is of Joe Barr chasing me with a wee pink baby mouse which had fallen out of its nest and escaped from the corn stack. I have been petrified of mice ever since.

In preparation for threshing day, Mum brought out the big Delft mugs and soup plates for dinner. There could be eight to ten hungry men around the kitchen table. A large pot of Arran Victory potatoes was placed in the middle of the table and a good helping of soup made from shin was served, with extras available. This was washed down with buttermilk, followed by a bowl of rice pudding and muscatel raisins, which are difficult to come by nowadays, or stewed apples.

July was usually haymaking month and back then, the weather seemed to be more clement with mild balmy days. Drying the hay never seemed to be a problem. The farming industry is, of course, very dependent on the weather for potato harvesting, cereal growing, silage and haymaking, as well as the turnout of the cattle to grass in the spring. Favourable weather puts the farmer in a good mood and makes life much easier.

The weather seemed sunnier in the summers when I was a child. We put on ankle socks at Easter and didn't wear long socks again until we went back to school in the autumn. I also vividly remember courting couples making a *'lover's nest'* in the long grassy ditches along the rural roads. No such comforts as the back seat of a car in those days (the early fifties), and the sunny weather seemed to last forever when we were young and carefree.

I remember Norman telling me about a dreadful windstorm in the fifties, when a big field of corn stooks on their hill was blown across the back lane and the ears of corn were threshed with just the stalks of straw left behind. I have my mum's record of a dreadful storm more recently in 1984. She wrote: *'[A] storm of wind came on Wednesday January 11, and lasted for three days. It was followed by a severe frost on January 16, and the thaw set in on Saturday January 21.'* I also recall a fierce storm of wind and rain which peaked on Boxing Day 1998 and brought down trees in its wake. Our back lane was blocked with fallen trees.

There were some years of severe frost recorded as well as windstorms. 1945 was one such year. The River Bann was frozen over at Bannfield, now Coleraine's Tesco. It was reported to be thirty degrees below zero and there is a photograph in the community archives showing lots of skaters on the frozen river.

In February of 1947, there was heavy snow. This was the year after I was born. It was the coldest and harshest in living memory. Because the temperatures rarely rose above freezing point, the snow that had fallen across Ireland in January remained until the middle of March. Worse still, all subsequent snowfalls in February and March simply piled on top. And there was no shortage of snow that bitter winter. Of the fifty days between January 24th and March 17th, it snowed on thirty of them. The blizzard of February 25th was the greatest single snowfall on record and lasted for close on fifty consecutive hours, when it smothered the entire island of Ireland. The freezing temperatures solidified the snow, and the winds were so strong that they created snowdrifts of up to six-metres high, blocking roads and making travel impossible.

Norman's Aunty, Maggie Calvin, went into labour at an awkward time that year. The snow was level with the hedges, and in the freezing temperatures, she had to be transported to the maternity hospital on a tractor. It was an astonishing three weeks before the snow began to melt.

There is no doubt that our climate is changing. King Charles has been a game changer in championing the protection of the environment and climate change. He has left no stone unturned in investigating the causes of climate change and has found inspiration in surprising places. As I write this in June 2023, we have seen the hottest June on record in Ireland. Provisional data shows that June 2023 had a 16+ °C average temperature, exceeding the previous June record held for eighty-three years. The highest temperature in June was 29.6 °C. Research shows that this trend of warming temperatures will continue. In response we need to understand and plan for a changing climate. Global temperatures have hit record highs, underscoring the dangers of ever-increasing greenhouse gas emissions generated from burning fossil fuels. This year has seen many wildfires across the world and the latest data confirms what we have long feared — forest fires are becoming more widespread, burning twice as much tree cover as they did twenty years ago.

We can all access the National Severe Weather Warnings Archives (NSWWA), which include some useful key elements that include colour — red, amber and yellow. We can also observe the warning service for rain, thunderstorms, wind, snow, lightning, ice and fog in the various regions of Great Britain and Ireland.

My Dad certainly wasn't a meteorologist, but his weather predictions were fairly accurate. Many old farmers had their own unique ways of predicting the weather and they were often correct. When cattle seek the corner of a field or lie down in a group, a severe storm is imminent. When dogs eat grass, rain is coming. If there is dew on the grass in the morning, chances are it won't rain that day. If the smoke goes straight up out of the chimney, you will have a good day. If the smoke curls and wisps around the chimney, then rain is on the way. If it rains before seven, it will clear before eleven. If the birds build their nests high in the trees, it's a sign of good weather to come. Cats will clean their ears before rain. The louder the frogs, the more the rain. Bats flying around in the evening indicate fair weather. With three nights dewless, 'twill rain, you're sure to see. A red sky at night is a shepherd's delight. A red sky in the morning is a sailor's warning. If there's a ring around the moon, rain will come in the next three days. If there is enough blue in a cloudy sky to back a man's waistcoat, the sun will soon come out. There is evidence that if you spend enough time outside in the soil, your body will tell you when something certain is approaching and give you signs such as sore knees before a change in the weather or before a rainstorm. My mum had severe arthritis and she certainly could tell by her pain, that bad weather was at hand.

We always had a glass barometer which hung on the hall wall. Each morning as Dad stepped off the stairs, he went across the hall and tapped it. When it went back, it was a sign of bad weather and when it moved forward it predicted that good weather was on the way. He would say gleefully, *"The glass is going up today."*

Haymaking was before the crazy idea of silage was invented. My dad's Uncle Alex made his annual pilgrimage from Glasgow each year for the haymaking season. He was very tall and had a lovely mild Scottish brogue. We had no baler, so it was all worked by hand. It was put into hand cocks, which were a conical shape, then in a few days, into tramp cocks. During the final process, they were slipped on to a flat trailer and taken into a barn in the farmyard. I remember, on most days, Uncle Alex seemed to develop a thirst mid-afternoon when he sent my elder brothers to McCaughern's pub a mile away at Culcrow, for a few bottles of Guinness. The black stuff was duly delivered and placed on the shady side of the hay cocks, ready on tap for anyone who needed a coolant.

Uncle Jamie was Dad's bachelor uncle and came sometimes to help on the farm and stayed for a few days. My prankster Dad often said there was *"a slate missing."* Unbeknown to Jamie, Dad placed Mum's fox fur at the bottom of his bed. When he felt it, it almost gave him a heart attack, and he came flying down the stairs in a frenzied state of hysteria.

Dad talked about some of the pranks he and friends got up to in their youth. Such as putting a heavy jute bag over the chimney of a thatched house or tying a string to a door knocker and then hiding so that when the occupant went to the door no one was there.

Dad had a great repertoire of sayings. When we had sibling rivalry, he would often say, *"Birds in their little nests agree. It is a shameful sight, when members of one family fall out and chide and fight."* Another gem was, *"A toast - here's tae you and your folk, no forgettin' us and our folk. If iver us and our folk ran across you and your folk, you and your folk would be as guid to us and our folk as us and our folk were to you and your folk."* A favourite toast was *'D.V.W.P.D.N.I,'* which stood for: *'God Willing, weather permitting and the devil not interfering'.* When he raised a glass he would say, *"Up with it, in with it, God work His will with it".*

The following was a conundrum: *'The cuckoo, the tataloo, the leveret and the lark. The marsh snipe, the heather bleet. how many birds?'* It is only three birds - cuckoo and tataloo are the same, as are the marsh snipe and the heather bleat, the lark is a bird, and the leveret is a young hare. Another one that caught out many when said quickly was: Londonderry, Cork and Kerry. Spell that without an R. Because of his birth in Caheny, Dad had a particular liking for this adaptation of a poem:

> *'Oul Kilrea for drinking tay*
> *Maghera for Brandy*
> *Moneydig's a stinking hole*
> *But Caheny is the dandy'.*

On Dad's eightieth birthday, all the neighbours and friends gathered at Woodlands for a party. It was a packed house, and he was the star of the show. I compiled the following poem in his honour:

OUR DAD

> *In the year nineteen hundred and eight*
> *At a place of great renown*
> *... a pretty blue-eyed boy was born ...*
> *The pride of Caheny town*
>
> *His mother said he was slow to talk,*
> *So to the doctor she went.*
> *But the doctor said, "He'll talk alright"*
> *And on her way she was sent*
>
> *When he started school at Moneydig,*
> *Oh what a dreadful plight.*
> *He naturally learnt to write with his left,*
> *But was told to use his right*
>
> *He still is really left-handed*
> *And to this very day*
> *He only has three-quarters of a thumb*
> *Because he chopped the rest away*

And when he was long past Santa,
He still hung his sock on the bed,
But in the morning he discovered
There was peat inside instead

He had an Uncle Jamie
The wisest of the clan,
If Dad wanted any kind of job done,
Then Jamie was "yer man"

So Dad and he were great pals,
But at cycling they hadn't a clue.
They collided at a corner,
Jamie shouts "I'm killed, are you?"

In the hungry early thirties,
When times were very hard,
Dad left Moville for the USA
Where no working lad boy was barred

The Bronx, Manhattan and Brooklyn
Were new names to the Irish lad
Where skyscrapers reached to heaven
And they called a taxi a cab

Then down he went to the underground,
And found a job we're told,
He worked late into the evenings
To line his pockets with gold

To go to Madison Square Gardens
Was young Tommy's chief intent,
And watch the sparring partners
Box each other with contempt

For seven years he toiled there,
But the pull of the Emerald Isle,
Made him long fondly for his homeland
And the eyes with the Irish smiles

So back he came to Ireland
And bought this farm at Knockaduff,
Where he wore his bachelor buttons …
But three years were long enough

Then he headed across the country,
To a place close to Ringsend
Down a very long lane he found a wife
Who his socks and things would mend

The knot is still tied tightly
No happier couple you'd find
"He eats too much," she says. "You'll burst."
He says, "That's a constant rhyme."

To rear the five of us, you know,
He worked hard as any man
And we all do appreciate
The labours of his hand

It's great to have you one and all,
To join family, neighbours and friends.
Without your presence, it would be in vain
For on you the fun depends

And so we're gathered here tonight
To toast eighty happy years.
We wish Dad well, we wish him health
Can we all say, 'three good cheers.'

Chapter 4

Derry's Walls

The 12th of July was always a special date on the calendar in my youth. Dad was a member of Caheny Flute Band and was made an Orangeman in Caheny 'League of Legends' (LOL 271). That always reminds me of the story of a wee Sunday School pupil being asked by his teacher: *"Who made you?" "I'm not made, but me da's made,"* he replied. The parade for his lodge was always held in a town in south County Londonderry. He always took the boys, while Mum and I held the fort at home. Off they went with their pristine white shirts and polished shoes to keep the Orange Order worthy of respect.

My husband, Norman was also a member of a Lodge - Loughanreagh, Lodge 909, and our boys were in the accordion band. The first year we were married, he asked me to polish his shoes. I completed the task, albeit unwillingly and asked his mother if she hadn't taught him to polish his own shoes. *"Ah well, I thought it was better for me to clean them than him go out among people with his dirty shoes,"* she replied.

The Orange Order is believed to be a Christ-centred global organisation, with a membership spanning many continents. The membership is drawn from all reformed denominations and a wide spectrum of political allegiance; it comprises men, women, boys and girls, who gather on the 12th July to celebrate the Revolution of 1688–1690 and King William III's victory at the Battle of the Boyne in 1690, when his army fought King James II. The leader of James' Army was Patrick

Sarsfield. William of Orange, who was a Dutchman by birth, would later reign as King of England, Scotland and Ireland, until his death in 1702. His wife, Mary was the eldest daughter of King Charles of England, Scotland and Ireland. He won the battle and captured the cities of Cork and Dublin. King James II left Ireland for France.

This laid the foundation of democratic government, and within a century was to provide inspiration for Ulster emigrants who travelled to the New World to again stand for basic civil liberties in the American Revolution of 1776. During that war, one third of the American armies consisted of men from Ulster. Their leader, George Washington, said, *"If defeated everywhere else, I will make my stand for liberty with the Scots Irish of my native Virginia."*[4] Interestingly, the US Constitution and Bill of Rights were shaped by an Ulsterman.

Eighteen town and city venues will this year, in 2023, be playing host to processions to mark the 333rd anniversary of the Battle of the Boyne, and more than 50,000 people will descend on Coleraine's celebration this year. Coleraine always welcomes lodges and bands from County Donegal each year. The rolling hills and splendid coastline provide the backdrop for the annual *Rossnowlagh Parade*, which takes place on the Saturday preceding the *Twelfth Parade* in the picturesque setting of County Donegal. There are usually upwards of fifty lodges and bands taking part. It is an impressive sight as the parade snakes through the narrow country roads, which are thronged with spectators, as it makes its way to the spectacular shoreline of Donegal. The annual parade is renowned for its friendly atmosphere and proves to be a lovely family day out.

Special Orange services are held each year in July to remember those who gave their lives in defence of civil liberties, including at the Battle of the Somme, where on the first day of the conflict, the British Army suffered huge casualties including 5,000 Ulstermen.

The 12th of August was also a special day for us as a family each year and was always celebrated on the 2nd Saturday in August, when our

---

[4] George Washington, founding father of the United States. Quote taken from Ulster-Scots Agency.

family drove to Londonderry where the Apprentice Boys of Derry gathered for the celebration of the Relief of Derry and the events of 1689. Dad didn't count himself a Harry Lauder [5] of a singer, but on the car journey to Londonderry on August 12th, we always had a rendering of his usual party piece, *Derry's Walls*, as he sang his heart out at the top of his voice:

> *"But fight and don't surrender,*
> *But call when duty calls,*
> *With heart and hand and sword and shield,*
> *We'll guard old Derry's walls."*

And that is just the chorus.

The online source, Wikipedia, contains the following about the siege: *'The siege of Derry was the first major event in the Williamite War in Ireland. The siege was preceded by an attempt against the town by Jacobite forces in 1688 that was foiled when 13 apprentices shut the gates of Derry city. This was an act of rebellion against James II. The second attempt began on April 18, 1689 when James himself appeared before the walls with an Irish army led by Jacobite and French officers. The town was summoned to surrender but refused'.* [6] The siege began. The besiegers tried to storm the walls but failed. They then resorted to starving Derry. During the siege Jacobite forces constructed a boom across the narrows of the river Foyle to prevent ships delivering supplies to the blockaded city. They raised the siege and left when supply ships broke through to the town. The siege lasted 105 days from the 18th of April to the 1st of August 1689. 30,000 protestant people held the walled city of Londonderry in the face of the Catholic King James II, until the relief fleet with a ship called *Mountjoy*, broke through the boom across the river Foyle on July the 28th. The Jacobite forces commenced their retreat on August the 1st, 1689. During the siege, disease and hunger took hold within the city. It became evident that the city needed to be relieved. Some 4,000 of its garrison of 8,000 are said to have died during this siege.

---

[5] Sir Harry Lauder (1870-1950) was a famous Scottish singer and comedian. He achieved international success with Music Hall performances singing *'Keep Right on to the End of the Road and Roaming in the Gloaming.*
[6] https://en.wikipedia.org/wiki/Siege_of_Derry

Another online source, *Hardships From the Garrison at Derry provides more detail about the terrible consequences of the siege: 'Starvation and disease caused by hunger and privation, were the most formidable enemies of the garrison. Famine slew more than the cannon of the enemy. On July 8th 1689, a pound of meal, a pound of tallow and two pounds of aniseeds were distributed to each man. The meal was mixed with tallow and ginger; pepper and aniseeds were added and the whole made into pancakes, which must have proved to be despicable fare, but no better could be obtained. Later in the month, essentials of a much more nauseous kind were anxiously sought and would usually be bought at a high price. A peck* [7] *of meal would easily bring six shillings; butter, 6 pence a pound; a dog 6 shillings, and the blood of a horse 2 pence a quart. A good cat would draw four and sixpence, a rat a shilling and a mouse sixpence in the last week of the siege. No man who survived that fearful trial ever forgot his experience of Derry.'* [8] And we groan about the cost-of-living crisis today!

My Dad's uncle, Fisher Robinson, lived in York Street in the waterside area of the city and we were always invited to park at his house and walk over the Craigavon Bridge to the city centre. The celebrations began at midnight on the morning of the second Saturday in August, with the firing of a cannon from the walls. It is fired each year by members of the organising parent club with assistance from a cannon crew from the crimson players. The following morning, they parade the walls. One of the main events is the thanksgiving service in St Columb's Cathedral, at 10:30 a.m. The service is open to everyone, all brethren, band members and members of the public are welcome to attend. 12 noon sees the main parade of the day and every club parading around the city. It is one of the biggest pageants in Northern Ireland with approximately 10,000 Apprentice Boys accompanied by over 100 bands. The finale usually ends at 5:00 p.m. with the colours returned to the Memorial Hall and the general committee's band playing *Derry's Walls* followed by the National Anthem.

---

[7] Peck = 9.09 litres or 2 dry gallons.
[8] https://www.libraryireland.com/Derry1689/IV-21.php

Chapter 5

Local Fellowships

Saturday night was bath night in a galvanised bath-pan in front of the Rayburn Royal Range, and that was deemed sufficient until the following week. Then a portion of Scripture was read in front of the fire.

Sundays were set aside for the things of God. Sunday School preceded church. Afternoon Sunday School was at Culcrow School, organised by the Ballylaggan Reformed Presbyterian Church. Many of the psalms were memorised along with familiar choruses such as follows:

1. *When He cometh, when He cometh,*
   To make up His jewels,
   All His jewels, precious jewels,
   His loved and His own.

   Refrain

   Like the stars in the morning,
   His bright crown adorning,
   They shall shine in their beauty,
   Bright gems for His crown.

2. *He will gather, He will gather*
   The gems for His kingdom;
   All the pure ones, all the bight ones,
   His loved and His own.

Refrain

3. *Little children, little children,*
   Who love their Redeemer,
   Are the jewels, precious jewels,
   His loved and His own.

Refrain [9]

The Aghadowey Girls' Auxiliary took place weekly under the leadership of Margaret Henderson, (née Hegarty). She personified Christianity to its fullest. For many years she organised camps to Guysmere, Castlerock and Bushmills Grammar School. One of the highlights was a visit to her grand residence at Rushbrook for afternoon tea. Those were the days when this was a novelty.

I always cycled the five miles to church organisations albeit by different routes. Once I went by Torrens's corner and met Elizabeth Warnock. Another time I went through Gillespie's farmyard, over the stepping stones across the Aghadowey River, up the Collins Lane to Moneybrannon and on to Lisnamuck where I met my friend Norma Black for the remainder of the journey.

Sometimes, I came home by Rusky where I passed Lizard Manor, the home of the Right Honourable Phelim Robert Hugh O'Neill (1904 –1994). The 2nd Baron Rathcavan was a politician in Northern

---

[9] Author: William Cushing, 1856, USA, (1823-1903).

Ireland and a hereditary peer in the British House of Lords. Lizard Manor was in the Stronge[10] family until it came into the possession of the Right Honourable Phelim O'Neill in 1953. He lived there until 1978, when he moved to County Mayo. The house was a large, two-storey, mid-Victorian property and described as *'a first-class dwelling that consisted of twenty-two rooms and possessed a large number of outbuildings, including two stables and two coach houses, five cow sheds, a boiling house, a barn and a large walled garden.'* [11]

Wikipedia gives further detail about Phelim himself: *'Phelim studied at Eton College before joining the Royal Artillery. He became a major during World War II and was elected to Westminster for the Ulster Unionist Party in the 1952 North Antrim by-election, when he succeeded his father. In 1958, he was appointed High Sheriff of Antrim, and in 1969, he briefly served as Minister of Education before becoming the Minister of Agriculture. He had six children; his son, Hugh O'Neill, was chairman of the Northern Tourist Board for some time and his cousin, Captain Terence O'Neill, was the Prime Minister of Northern Ireland between 1963 and 1969. The O'Neill dynasty goes back to the 1600s.'* [12]

I admired Phelim's plummy accent with all its airs and graces. But that aside, he had a wonderful personality and style, and made me most welcome and always gave a kind donation to my charity. Because I was underage, I had to decline his offer of a sherry on each visit.

However, Bridget, Phelim's wife was a rather peculiar individual. She was eccentric in appearance and manner, always wore baggy sweaters and often looked dishevelled. She had a pet monkey which entered and exited the house via the kitchen window. On one occasion it

---

[10] A Sir Norman Stronge was a junior officer in the British Army during WWI where he fought in the Battle of the Somme and was awarded the Military Cross. After the war he became speaker of the House of Commons for twenty-three years. While watching television with his son in Tynan Abbey, their home, he was shot and killed at the age of eighty-six, along with his son James, aged forty-eight, by the Provisional IRA in 1981. Their home with all its treasures was burnt to the ground. The extensive estate once amounted to 8,000 acres. The ruin was demolished in 1998, having stood for 249 years.'

[11] https://lordbelmontinnorthernireland

[12] https://en.wikipedia.org/wiki/Phelim_O%27Neill,_2nd_Baron_Rathcavan

became unwell, and Bridget took it to the Ballymoney veterinary surgeon where she withdrew it from under her jumper. The vet had to consult his textbook to find out the normal temperature of a monkey. I think it is similar to a human.

During the summer, my teenage friends and I cycled around the neighbourhood collecting for the School of Deaf, Dumb and Blind at Jordanstown. We had our little record book to check the previous year's donations and a designated Saturday was arranged to collate the money at Miss Maggie Gilmore's little thatched cottage. She coordinated the project and invited us for the annual afternoon tea. This woman kept a goat to provide the milk for the house. The table was laid, and the tea was infused. Everything was going okay until the goat's milk was added to the tea. It gave the tea a yellow/orangey hue and a taste that was pungent to say the least. What were we to do? Intervention saved the day. Miss Gilmore went out to the kitchen to replenish the teapot and with haste two of the girls, who shall remain anonymous, watered a convenient pot plant with the offending refreshment.

The youth group organised parties in the church hall where Jack Smith was the resident musician with his accordion. As we swung the corners, where he was placed, he often made a lunge for the girls as they went by. When someone requested a lift home with Jack, he always had the same reply: *"I canna tak ye, I hae a load o' wee Hoggs to lee hame".*

Chapter 6

Home Cooking

D ad and Mum put much emphasis on work ethics, diligence and charity, in the belief that these had a moral benefit and an inherent ability, virtue and value to strengthen character, although it was mainly carried out doing chores around the farm and farmyard. Mum was of average height and had brown wavy hair. She had a passion for style and always looked good in her attire. She always had a matching handbag and wore stiletto heels until she was in her eighties. She taught me the rudiments of housekeeping, cooking and baking. She was a wonderful homemaker, baker and gardener. She had green fingers and whatever the cuttings she planted — they grew.

Soup was made weekly, and a hen was taken from the flock and trussed. A dish of methylated spirits was set alight on the floor and after plucking the feathers, the down was singed off. I was very young when I took the innards from the carcass. The gizzard, heart, neck and liver were put into a saucepan with the chicken, peas, barley and seasoning, all to make a pot of wholesome broth. There is no tasty soup like that nowadays. I was taught how to bone a chicken, stuff it and make it into a roll for a buffet table:

HOW TO DEBONE A CHICKEN:

1. *With the chicken in a prone position, break the thigh bone by grabbing the leg with one hand and holding down the backbone against the chopping board.*

2. *Rock the leg back and forth while pushing down on the backbone until the thigh bone breaks off and starts to move freely.*

3. *Feel where the bone joint is attached and push down on that point. Repeat that step for the other thigh bone. Using a pair of kitchen scissors snip the bone off the meat.*

4. *This will create an incision-like opening that will be the starting point for separating the bone from the meat. Snip deeply enough for the spoon to have a good grab when you start scooping. Using a spoon and scooping and cutting motions, work your way between the bone and the meat to separate them. A pair of kitchen scissors may be necessary if the spoon won't go through.*

5. *Turn the chicken over and do the same on the other side. Once you feel the bone has been separated from the meat, slowly pull it out and use the scissors as necessary to separate the bone from the meat.*

6. *Et voila! Now you have your deboned chicken and you're also a certified chicken orthopaedic surgeon. It can be stuffed with bread stuffing, sausage meat and strips of bacon, sown up into a roll and cooked in a moderate oven for 1½ hours. It's delicious sliced hot or cold.*

The griddle was used to bake soda bread, pancakes and potato bread known as fadge or slims, and the excess flour was swept off with a goose's wing.

Ling was a popular fish for salting, it was hung below the stairs and a slice was cut off when necessary, then it was steeped in water to take out excess salt, before it was cooked in milk — it was delicious. It can still be sourced in Glass's fruit shop in Bushmills.

Churning day took place weekly, and the butter was kept in a mesh safe in the backyard along with the meat. Milk was stored in a large crock surrounded with water and placed on the stone floor in the pantry. It was the fifties, so there was no cultured buttermilk in those days. When you had a glass of buttermilk, it was the real thing, with droplets of butter floating on the top.

Despite Mum's busy schedule, she loved entertaining visitors. It was usually high tea, with a nice salad and cold meat. Ox tongue was a delicacy, which was boiled, skinned, then squeezed into a pudding bowl with a weight set on top before being finely sliced when it was cold.

When there was a death or any trouble in our neighbourhood, Dad and Mum were on the doorstep of the grieving family laden with food of every kind. Mum's apple creams, meringues, vanilla slices and her prize-winning sponges were legendary around the countryside. She never possessed an electric mixer until much later in life, all was done by hand.

PRIZE SPONGE RECIPE

Ingredients:

4 medium eggs

3 ozs caster sugar

3 ozs self-raising flour

A pinch of salt

Vanilla essence

Method:

Beat eggs and sugar until thick and pale. Gently fold in dry ingredients and spread into 2 lined 8-inch cake tins and bake at 180°C for 15 minutes.

Mum won the *Home Industries Cup* for three consecutive years, when she attained the highest points in the home industries section at Coleraine Show, but she was not allowed to compete after winning the cup outright. When she presented a replacement trophy *(The Diana Hogg Cup)* she then persuaded me to enter in all twenty-four sections. I was a busy mum with four young children, but I thought I'd give it a go. History repeated itself when I won Mum's cup outright after also attaining the highest points in all sections for three years. I took early retirement!

When Norman and I became engaged in 1967, it was customary to invite the future in-laws to tea. A summer evening was arranged. All was under control and the table groaned with *'all kinds of everything'.* A distant cousin of Dad's had bequeathed her estate to him and that included a lovely, solid-silver teapot. The specimen was never used, but on this special occasion the teapot got an airing for the first time. Everything was ready and the guests were ushered to their seats at the well-laden table. I *'wet'* the tea and set it on the cooker. And then, horror of horrors, the silver teapot began melting before my eyes. I quickly picked it up and proceeded to pour the tea; the *faux pas* went unseen by the guests. There was damage done to the base, but a well-known silversmith in Coleraine saved the day and was able to repair it. He melted and fused the teapot base until the defect was almost unnoticeable. In my ignorance, I hadn't realised silver melted.

I also inherited an old 8-day school wall clock made by J W Johnston, Coleraine, which keeps perfect time to this day. As it strikes loudly every hour, I always remove the pendulum when my son and daughter-in-law come to stay.

Mum and Dad always enjoyed receiving and entertaining guests; making them feel welcome, showing regard and always ensuring that they had a positive experience when visiting our home.

ENTERTAINING ANGELS UNAWARES.

'Do not forget to entertain strangers, for by so doing some have unwittingly entertained angels without knowing it' Hebrews 13:2 (NIV).

The story is told of a young soldier who had been away fighting in Vietnam. He phoned his parents in San Francisco. *"I am coming home,"* he said, *"but I have a favour to ask, I want to bring a friend home." "Sure,"* they replied, *"We'd love to meet him." "There is something you should know,"* their son said. *"He was hurt badly in the fighting. He stepped on a landmine and lost an arm and a leg and has nowhere to go. I want him to come and live with us."*

There was silence for a moment. *"You don't know what you are asking. Someone with such a handicap would be a terrible burden. We think you should just come home and forget about him. He'll find a way to live on his own."* At that, the son hung up and his parents heard nothing more from him. Sometime later they received a phone call from the San Francisco police who advised them that their son had died after fall from a building. The grief-stricken parents flew to San Francisco and were taken to the city morgue to identify his body. To their horror they discovered that he had only one arm and one leg.

The Lord wants us to love people with the same unconditional love that He has for us, so be very careful today who you refuse to welcome into your home. You may be entertaining an angel unawares.

Chapter 7

Dress to Impress

The rural tailor was not only a man, but a magician, or a creator, for he transformed a man by clothing him in fine clothes fit for a nobleman. Today, people are not so particular about their clothes as they once were. Today men who hold important positions - doctors, professors at the universities, even our clergymen, do not dress up, even for important occasions. I'm probably old-fashioned, but it was nice to see a well–dressed man in my youth. Many years ago, men who held high-ranking positions dressed smartly, some even wore silk hats and frock coats, as they were called then. But there is another side to this philosophy of clothes. The tailor cannot clothe the soul of man, and the soul is more important.

Rural tailoring has gone down in the annals of history. One such man is still etched in my memory. Alec Downs and his daughter, Nan and son, Jack, ran their tailoring workshop from the back room of their house at Coolyvenny, Aghadowey. Nan continued her expertise in the alteration department of Tweedy Acheson at The Diamond, when her dad retired in the 1970s.

When my mum and my dad had clothes made, I went along as a young observer and was intrigued by the set-up of Downs' Tailor Shop. Alec served his apprenticeship at Willie Ramsey's of Dromore, Aghadowey, Coleraine, a few miles from his home. On Willie's retirement Alec set up business on his own account at his dwelling house — no planning application was necessary in those days. I was intrigued during my visits with my parents and fascinated by the irons in the oven at the ready to press the suits. Some of them weighed sixteen to twenty pounds. There was always an assortment of scissors on the large cutting table: cutting scissors, trimming scissors and hole-cutters (for buttonholes). Another important tool was the bodkin and each tailor had one of these. It was a small piece of equipment made of bone, which was about half the size of a pencil, and it had a point. It was used to push out the corners, shape buttonholes and take out basting or tacking. It was said that the bodkin was taken out of the back of the tailor's neck so that he would not get cramp because he'd been sitting for so long with his head bent forward. Funnily enough most tailors walked straight with a very upright posture and certainly Alec and Nan Downs walked upright and had good deportment, which was also evident in their daily lives. They were lifetime members of Dromore Presbyterian Church which has sadly closed this past year.

Alec was meticulous in every way. Nan often said he made his bed perfectly every morning. In those days it would have been made with sheets, blankets, a bedspread and an eiderdown or quilt. It is much easier to throw a duvet over a bed today. He was a gentle giant with square shoulders, a glint in his brown eyes and a gentle demeanour. When a customer came in, Alec was equipped with a tape measure around his neck, a square, a yard stick and chalk. Each customer was unique to Alec and he made his own patterns to the customer's specific requirements. He matched checks so well and asked Nan's help in looking at shadowy checked materials to make sure they were exactly right. As well as Dad's suits, Alec made Mum's costumes — that's what they called women's suits. I didn't drool over them - they were made of men's suiting material, and although it was fine cloth, I thought they were not for women. A hand-stitched flat hat was made to tone with the 'costume' and the ensemble was complete.

The farming fraternity were good customers and came from all arts and parts of County Londonderry, County Antrim, and beyond. Summer was the busiest time of the year, especially around the 12th of

July when Nan said her dad never went to bed so that he could fulfil the orders. He catered for weddings, with black jackets and striped trousers.

Work satisfaction mattered much more than money to Alec Downs. When a satisfied customer donned his worsted suit with the hand stitching around the collar and lapels to make it sit well, Nan recalled how proud her father felt when he saw the finished article on a very happy customer. There were the misfits too, but Alec customised the suit to fit a short leg or some other irregularity. These problems proved difficult sometimes but were all part and parcel of a tailor's work.

The Downs' household was well known for laughter, but never anything untoward, just merriment; there was always someone singing. Friends and neighbours often gathered at the end of a day's work and told stories and played draughts. Both Alec and his son were brilliant draught players; many games were played and won in the workshop on a winter's night.

During the long summer evenings, the game of horseshoes was played at the end of the Managher Road. Legend states that horseshoes originated in Ancient Rome over 2,000 years ago. The story goes that while out on deployment, Roman soldiers collected horseshoes discarded by their officers and pitched them towards a target. The Wikipedia entry under *'Horseshoe (game)'* states the following: *'It's a game played between two people using four horseshoes and two targets set in grass or a sandbox area. The game is played with the players having alternate turns tossing horseshoes at stakes in the ground, which are traditionally placed forty feet apart.'* [13] I believe, because it was generational, the game has declined in popularity nowadays.

Sadly, with the passage of time and the demise of the rural tailor, the country is much poorer. All I can say is that I have many happy and precious memories of the Downs' tailoring family at Coolyvenny — a well-known tailoring family who lived only a couple of miles from my home in Knockaduff.

---

[13] https://en.wikipedia.org/wiki/Horseshoes_(game)

Chapter 8

Our First Holiday

I t was 1963, when two friends and I set off to Butlins for our first holiday. Mosney was the first Butlins' holiday camp outside the UK, and it became a resounding success. Although Mosney was much smaller than its British counterparts, it included the trademark chalets, swimming pool, large dining room, theatre and amusement arcade. The *Redcoats* were easily recognised as guides with their smart red uniforms. It was a cheap, affordable holiday for families, and as we thought, the experience of a lifetime. Billy Butlin had brought his tried and tested holiday formula for young singles from the UK. It was such a success that people from all over the country came to it. When the camp opened the Catholic Church became extremely angry. *The Catholic Standard* newspaper stated clearly that: *"Holiday camps are an English idea and are alien and undesirable in an Irish Catholic country."* [14]

The Irish community ignored the church's concerns for their moral welfare, but Billy Butlin, wary of how people used to listen to the church in those days, built a Catholic Church in the camp to please the hierarchy. Butlin sold the camp as a going concern in 1983. The camp now accommodates asylum seekers from fifty different countries.

It was a very memorable holiday where Scottish lassies and the guys from St Johnston Donegal were a big hit. One friend was a bit of an obstacle, having tacked her pleated skirts to keep them in shape and the tacking thread had to be carefully removed each time we

---

[14] https://en.wikipedia.org/wiki/Billy_Butlin

ventured out. Perfection for her was the order of the day, while we were '*champing at the bit*' to get out for the evening.

It was August 1964, when a friend and I went on our first continental holiday. Rimini in north Italy was our destination. We set off from Victoria Coach Station enroute to Manston Airport to fly to Ostend. On arrival we met our continental coach and set out for Brussels, on through Liège and Aachen to Cologne where we crossed the Rhine with its busy river traffic. After dinner we settled down in the coach for the night drive along the smooth autobahn to Frankfurt, Ulm and Munich. Unfortunately, we were seated beside the toilets and while the courier continually sprayed air freshener, the stench was rather overpowering. The cure was worse than the disease. Not surprising though, on a budget holiday at £65 for ten days. We stopped at Innsbruck then over the Brenner Pass and then it was down the plains of northern Italy to Rimini on the Italian Riviera with its sandy beaches stretching for twelve miles along the blue sea. We were glad of a good night's sleep and fresh air. The next day we set off in search of a new continental experience and we weren't disappointed. With 3,000 years of history, we found Rimini fascinating. One day we met up with a couple of Italian guys on the beach. Ignoring our parents' advice not to separate, we decided to go our separate ways and meet back at our hotel for dinner. My friend went off in a sports car and I hopped on the back of a motorbike. On the continent, darkness descends very quickly, and my chauffeur decided I should see Rimini by night, which was spectacular. The starry sky, the balmy air and the panoramic sight of the city lights from the hilltop above Rimini took my breath away. For the moment I forgot my return arrangements and when I did, I quickly asked my companion to hasten back to the hotel where I found my friend safely deposited and a tad worried, anxiously awaiting my safe return. All was well, we never had a disagreement throughout the holiday, and we remain best friends to this day. On the tenth day of our holiday, we boarded our plane for the return flight to Manston, then on to London and the end of a truly memorable experience.

From then on, we settled down with our respective boyfriends and the holidays were over.

Chapter 9

My Norman

Apart from Norman Calvin McClelland's birth on May 29th, there were many significant happenings in 1938. In the same timeframe, Adolf Hitler invaded neighbouring Austria in March, and shortly afterwards forced a carefully supervised popular vote that favoured unification with Nazi Germany, with a robust 99.7 per cent in favour. The Anschluss was clearly an act of naked aggression. Then in October, Adolf Hitler's Army marched into Sudetenland in Czechoslovakia. In September, Hitler met with British Prime Minister, Neville Chamberlain and stated his demand that Czechoslovakia yield Sudetenland, a region with a large German population, to Nazi Germany. On November 9th and 10th, Nazi leaders unleashed a series of pogroms against the Jewish population in Germany and its recently incorporated territories. This event was to become known as *Kristallnacht (Night of Broken Glass)* [15] because of the shattered glass that littered the streets after the vandalism and destruction of Jewish-owned businesses, synagogues and homes.

That year the British cabinet allowed 10,000 unaccompanied Jewish children into Britain in an action called *Kindertransport*.

Other significant events that occurred during 1938 include:

- *An underground explosion at Markham Colliery, Derbyshire that killed seventy-nine people.*

---

[15] https://en.wikipedia.org/wiki/Kristallnacht

- *Test cricket was televised for the first time.*

- *The Pay Act provided for paid annual leave and holidays in wage-related industries and for similar voluntary schemes in other employment.*

- *The Beano comic went on sale for the first time.*

- *RMS Elizabeth was launched in Clydebank. It was the largest ship in the world at that time.*

- *The first green belts began to be established in the UK, around Sheffield and London. They hadn't reached Northern Ireland at that stage.*

- *Paul Daniels, magician, was born in 1938, as was Baroness May Blood MBE, a Belfast politician.*

- *Diana Rigg was born in 1938, as well as David Dimbleby, the broadcaster and Richard Meade an equestrian.*

- *£100 in 1938, is worth £8,611.62 today.*[16]

Norman was the first-born child of Thomas and Ruby McClelland and was followed by two brothers Joseph (Joe) and Thomas (Tom). He inherited his height from his mother's Calvin genes and always walked tall and straight; he had fine wispy hair, which he held on to until he died. Like his mum and unlike most farmers, he had hands like velvet. Farming was in his blood from an early age. He often told me how he came home on his bike from Coleraine Inst at lunchtime to lie at the back of the hedge and watch an ewe lambing. His Latin teacher said to him, *"Norman didn't know enough Latin to cover a postage stamp."* Not very encouraging!

His Aunty Jean Calvin operated a wee confectionary/grocer's shop on Railway Road, Coleraine in the fifties, and, of course, the Institute

---

[16] Adapted from https://www.thepeoplehistory.com/1938.html

boarders got to know about it and Norman became the message boy operating a tuck shop at lunchtime. He was always a keen rugby player and went to Paris as an Inst team member. He also played soccer in the Irish Society team.

Very often the townies looked on the rural kids as country *'gulpins'* and thought them a tad weak. On one occasion, when Norman was showing off his baby tooth to his infant classmates, a street urchin knocked it out of his hand, set his foot on it, and smashed it into smithereens. There was to be no tooth fairy that day. Apparently, Norman didn't retaliate until many years later. He clearly remembered the incident and when an opportunity came up on the football pitch, he gave the offending opponent a painful kick on the shin. No red card was handed out and revenge was sweet.

Chapter 10

Humble Beginnings

It is said *'Love is blind, but marriage is an eye opener.'* I can identify with that statement, but for all the right reasons. Norman, unlike me, had a very big family circle; his mum was from a family of nine, although three died in childhood. There were always callers at Tullans, and Nana Ruby, Norman's mum, like my mum, was a great hostess, wonderful cook, baker, jam maker and needle woman. I have some of her lovely tapestries gracing our home. She was very tall, possessed an elegant and sophisticated poise, and had a gentle, kind and encouraging spirit to match her other attributes. She always looked good in her clothes and loved to be stylish. She was the last woman to wear a hat in Ballyrashane Church. Nana was quite a disciplinarian too, and our children received many a crack with her walking stick. Neighbours would call in frequently with the latest news. My mother-in-law would have made a great nurse, handling anything from a bloodied face to a broken limb, whereas I can't stand the sight of blood and go weak at the knees. She often recalled being asked by a neighbour in the district to lay out, prepare and dress a dead body for burial. How morbid was that? I don't know what the undertaker did.

Norman's grandfather came to Tullans from a farm at Dunalis, a townland between Macosquin and Articlave, about 5 miles from Coleraine, around 1890. It covered about thirty-three acres. A few years after he arrived, he married Mary Eliza Adams, a neighbour.

Tullans is translated from Irish *'Tollankille'*, meaning, *'the place of little hills.'* This is etched above our front door. I never thought Norman would accede to the Irish version, but he did. He had no option as it was already in place when he discovered it. Apparently, Norman's grandfather said that his father sent him to the clay hole at Tullans. Clay loams tend to be heavy and slow draining and are difficult to work when wet - the complete opposite to the free-draining loamy soil of Dunalis. My home farm at Knockaduff had a type of loamy soil like Dunalis. However, you become familiar with the land you work, and when other folk are tilling their land, you get used to being patient and waiting for two weeks before planting. Despite the delay in spring, it is very productive land.

Joseph McClelland, Norman's grandfather was elected an elder in Ballyrashane church in 1906. But declined the nomination.

Over the years the McClelland farm was increased in size by including a further thirty-three acres bought from John Stirling, Stanley Knowe, and Robert Boyle's farm, further in than McClelland's own farm. Our son, Ross, built a house on the steading. There was also a small holding bought from Soloman and Daniel Laverty which lay between their own farm and the road. The field, where Ian has built his house, was owned by Mayrs' family and was bought by Norman's dad.

One of Norman's great uncles emigrated to New Zealand and was never heard of again. Apparently, no one was surprised as he had a bad temper. Once, when his mother was ironing his detachable collar and it wasn't to his satisfaction, he threw it into the open fire. Thankfully that characteristic has all but disappeared from the ensuing generations.

Another of Norman's great uncles had an illustrious career in the field of science: Professor John McClelland, F.R.C., 1909, M.A., D.Sc., (RUI), M.A. (Cambridge), D. Sc., (Dublin), Professor of Experimental Physics (University College, Dublin), Commissioner of National Education, Ireland. He was born in 1870, into a family of eleven on a farm at Dunalis, and went by bicycle to Coleraine Academical Institution, which was five miles away, and then to Queen's College, Galway. His achievements were numerous. He earned the title of the first science scholar at Royal University for Galway; and was awarded a special prizeman M.A. Degree (RUI) in 1893. Among his other accomplishments he also gained an exhibition scholarship in 1894 and junior fellowship (RCI) in 1895; followed by fellowship in 1901, at Trinity College, Cambridge. He obtained a Cambridge Research Degree, at Cambridge in 1897. He was professor of physics at University College Dublin in 1900, and a member of the senate of the National University of Ireland and of the governing body of University College in 1908. He was secretary of the Royal Irish Academy and a member of the advisory council for Scientific and Industrial Research Publication and presented papers on physical subjects in various journals.

Professor John married a Coleraine woman, Ina Esdale, in 1901, and had two sons and three daughters and died at a relatively young age at his home, *Rostrevor* in Orwell Road, Rathgar, Dublin. His descendants have stayed with us on many occasions. His father was known to say, *"That John boy couldn't turn a beast in the yard."* Obviously, even at an early age his mind was set on academia rather than agriculture. His main form of recreation was golf.

From humble beginnings on a farm in County Londonderry, this young boy, educated at Coleraine Academical Institution made a name for himself in the field of science. I'm pleased that some of our family have followed in his footsteps in science, albeit at a slower pace.

Norman also went to Coleraine Academical Institution but had to curtail his education after completing his junior certificate, because his father had a heart attack. He didn't have the opportunity to go to Greenmount Agricultural College but joined Coleraine Young Farmers Club instead. From an early age he had an inherent eye for stock judging and became the unofficial vet in the neighbourhood, saving many farmers veterinary fees along the way.

It wasn't all work and no play for Norman. He was a keen rugby, football and badminton player, and was sought after for cattle and sheep judging roles in Ireland and mainland Great Britain. He represented Ulster on International judging teams on no less than six occasions and processed many medals to record his success.

He spent some periods in hospital throughout his lifetime. The first of many fractures to his limbs happened when he was starting a Fordson tractor with the crank handle, which bounced back and broke his wrist. On another occasion a straw bale that was being conveyed up an escalator fell off and landed on Norman's head. He was admitted to hospital and required traction to his neck for several weeks. He ended up in hospital many times during his lifetime. As a loving father, he disciplined his offspring and taught them right from wrong with calm words and actions. In our family dynamics, some needed more discipline than others.

He grew seed and ware potatoes extensively, and the proceeds from their sale enabled us to build our house without a mortgage. Aside from our main farmhand, Jim Campbell, we also had Jamie Coulter, a train driver, and George Stalford, a paramedic, who came to help on their days off. On inspection day we always waited with bated breath to receive the certificate that the potatoes had passed inspection and were ready for the transport lorry to take them to Coleraine docks for shipping. Unlike today, potatoes were the staple diet in every household and were a lucrative farm enterprise for many years. Diets have changed dramatically, and the humble spud has been replaced by savoury rice and pasta. Thankfully *Champ*, with the butter swimming round, is still an old-time favourite in our household.

The potato was even more important in the mid-1800s during the Great Famine. This was a period of starvation when the potato succumbed to a destructive blight disease known as Phytophthora. Potatoes were the predominant diet of the rural poor in Ireland. They were often salted or mixed with seaweed to provide variety from the sheer monotony of a diet based on a single ingredient. But they were incredibly nutritious and easy to grow on a small plot of land. Consequently, over time they started to displace barley, wheat and beans. Therefore, a failure of the potato crop was devastating. During the famine period between 1846 and 1849, one million people died and more than 300,000 people emigrated, with another 150,000–170,000 dying of famine related diseases. What made the famine so lethal in Ireland is that it lasted for such a long period, with each failed crop representing another period of devastation for people across the country. The famine was a tragedy that is part of our collective heritage, affecting both the unionist and nationalist population.

CHAPTER 11

Was I Wife Material?

Having two elder brothers who chaperoned me, I was allowed out on the social scene at sixteen. Church parties were followed by dances in Orange halls around the country. Flamingo took place in Ballymena on a Wednesday night, in the Arcadia Ballroom, Portrush, where a fellow bought you an orange or coke and escorted you up to the balcony where you watched the revellers down below, as they danced the night away. Main Street Presbyterian Hall always hosted a YFC dance on Boxing Night. Cloughmills Orange Hall had a Young Farmers Club dance where, as I have said earlier, I met my future husband. I still have the peach dress I wore on that first date.

Although the romance blossomed, I became rather unsettled and had a longing to spread my wings and go into the world of academia to pursue a career in agriculture. So, in the autumn of 1965, I left my job in Tweedy Acheson's and my application was accepted for an agricultural course for girls in Strabane. I joined twenty-five other girls from all over the province. They included civil servants and nurses, and the majority were farmers' daughters; all extremely friendly. With the increase in farm units in the sixties, particularly in poultry farming, the demand for personnel, capable of managing, or assisting in operating modern-sized units, was increasing. The principal assured us there would be a good number of openings for capable girls who were thoroughly versed in practical husbandry, particularly in poultry-keeping and dairying, and of course, opportunities in other fields, such as laboratories and hatcheries. Other subjects included general agriculture, veterinary science, farm management and account-keeping. They emphasised the business-like approach to farming, which is of paramount importance, even to this day. In home management a large amount of cooking practice was included in combined lecture and demonstration classes in preference to straight lectures. One very practical demonstration was how to cut up a lamb carcass, which was produced at the school farm. I can think of no better way to learn the cuts of meat than with a demonstration of this sort. I still remember them to this day. It was a very comprehensive and excellent course which has stood me in good stead as a farmer's wife. I attained first prize overall and the *Ministry of Agriculture Scholarship* to Loughry Agriculture College, Cookstown. I also won the award for best overall project completed at the course. We held our fifty-year reunion in 2015.

With gentle persuasion, Norman, who was my boyfriend at the time I won the Scholarship, thought it best that I decline the offer to go to Loughry in September, and instead get a job with a view to settling down as a farmer's wife. I think he imagined that in Cookstown I might forget about him. I did distance myself from him for a while, when I secured a management job in Biggars in Londonderry. It was a disused pork factory in Foyle Street where the Department of Agriculture Orchard House headquarters is now. The English manager fancied himself as an entrepreneur and converted the factory floor to accommodate cages for laying hens. Who could imagine in the sixties, conveyor belts taking the hen manure out to farmer's trailers lined up along Sugar House Lane in the centre of the *Maiden City*? There was a good market for the eggs, and it turned out to be a profitable enterprise.

Upon my arrival in the city, my boss arranged lodgings in the YWCA hostel in Clarendon Street where I met a girl from Port-Na-Blagh, Donegal. After some time, we moved to a flat in Pump Street and then to a larger flat in Magazine Street, overlooking the Bogside, where we welcomed Eileen's sister, who was a nurse, and two more colleagues, making our number up to five. We always had plenty of eggs and made every dish under the sun!

One night the three nurses arrived home from Altnagelvin Hospital, armed with surgical spirits and sterilized needles to perform 'surgery' on each other's ears. I declined the offer and didn't get my ears pierced until I was twenty-one. Three were successful and one had a festering ear for months. I hadn't learnt to drive at that stage and enrolled for driving lessons. The driving instructor initially took me to less busy places such as Sherriff's Mountain, and then progressed to Bogside, which was overlooked by our flat. When the day of the test arrived, I felt quite confident, until a dog ran out in front of me in Lecky Road in the Bogside and I made an emergency stop, causing the examiner to hit his forehead on the dashboard. There were no seatbelts in those days. I knew I was doomed, and he failed me - not because of the dog incident, but because I didn't make sufficient use of my mirrors. I managed to pass the second time around.

The nurses' dances over the river at Altnagelvin were escapes from our mediocre existence on the city side. I had weekends off, but no car, which proved difficult. However, on most Friday evenings I hitched a lift to Coleraine with great success; I met many characters and had great conversations along the way. I resumed my chores at the weekend in Knockaduff, with a few escapades thrown in for good measure.

In the flat someone introduced us to 'hookie'. We put glasses on a board, and they moved around, seemingly at will. One weekend when I was home, my flatmate Hazel rang me to say she felt like I did - that the game was satanic and dark. We decided not to play it again. At that stage in my life, I had an awareness of God, and I taught a Sunday School class, but God seemed distant, and wasn't a felt presence in my daily life.

One weekend Mum decided to make blackberry wine as there was an abundance of blackberries in the hedges. In those days the hedgerows were not trimmed as they are today so there was a bountiful harvest. Mum had followed the recipe and corked the bottles. It was two weeks into the fermentation when an explosion was heard in the sitting room. The six bottles had burst, and purple liquid was splattered over the whole room.

 In those days we gathered blackberries and sold them to Mrs Torrens's shop in Agivey. I think that was a better option than the wine-making exercise. The ginger wine at Christmas was always a great success. As I remember, it was made from a small bottle of concentrated ginger essence and no fermentation was necessary.

Spring was always the time to cleanse our bodies and so we had a spoonful of molasses with a sprinkling of sulphur on top. I always remember the repugnant taste of the yellow powder on the roof of my mouth.

CHAPTER 12

A Green Hill Far Away

Our flat in Derry was on the verge of the Bogside and overlooked the estate to the green hills beyond, reminding me of the famous hymn by Mrs Frances Alexander.[17] At Easter services throughout the land and even across the globe, one simple but haunting song will almost certainly be sung *There is a Green Hill Far Away, Without a City Wall.* The words were written in 1847, in a house in Strabane, County Tyrone, by one of the most remarkable Irish women of her day — Mrs Cecil Frances Alexander. Legend tells us that the green hill which inspired her to write this most popular of all Easter hymns was a hill which could be seen from the walls of Derry, and which is now obscured by the massive housing developments that make up the Bogside where I sat my driving test. Her hymns and poems made Mrs Alexander a celebrity. The composer Charles Gounod said of the hymn, *"The words set themselves to music."* Another admirer was Disraeli. Even the wry-humoured, Mark Twain, was impressed.

Today, the poetess is mainly remembered for hymns which she wrote specifically for children, such as *All Things Bright and Beautiful* and the Christmas Carol *Once in Royal David's City.* All were written in Milltown House in Strabane, which later formed part of the grammar school. At the time Mrs Alexander was Miss Fanny Humphreys and had yet to meet her future husband, a man destined, some say through her fame, to become archbishop of Armagh and primate of

---

[17] https://en.wikipedia.org/wiki/Cecil_Frances_Alexander

Ireland. Fanny came from a well-to-do, Anglo-Irish family and was born in Georgian Dublin. At the age of fifteen, she moved to Strabane when her father became an agent for the Marquis of Abercorn on the Baronscourt Estate in County Tyrone. She was very much the Victorian young woman, who devoted herself to charity, good works and poetry. Even her greatest admirers admit that much of her writing then, and much later, was 'sugary' and some of it downright bad. But she refined her talent when in 1848 she published what was to become a sacred classic, *Hymns for Little Children*. This contained the three famous hymns already mentioned above, and many more simple and pleasant ones. It became a best seller. Fanny donated the proceeds to establish a school for deaf and dumb children around Strabane. It became the Derry and Raphoe Institution for the Deaf and Dumb, originally providing board for twenty-nine children. It strived to remedy the neglect such afflicted children suffered. Expressing her satisfaction with the school she wrote:

> *"Oh happiness, who runneth o'er*
> *With God's good gifts in mercy given,*
> *Turn from their own abundant store*
> *To teach the dumb, the songs of Heaven."*

She was grief-stricken ten years later when a fire destroyed the school, claiming the lives of six of the children.

Times were hard in Ireland in 1850, when Fanny married William Alexander, a young curate. The Great Famine killed millions as did the typhus epidemic which followed. William Alexander almost died of the plague while he was ministering to his parishioners. The newly-weds encountered much poverty and despair around them when they moved to the Parish of Aghyaran, a remote district near Castlederg. Many stories of Fanny's good deeds have been recorded as she tramped across moor and fell with parcels of food for the poor. Daily she dressed the cancerous wound of a Roman Catholic neighbour. She also paid for the education of a young man who wanted to become a teacher. She was tough too, and had a sense of humour and wit, which the Ulster country folk appreciated. For instance, in contrast to some of her high-flown stanzas, she wrote a powerful ballad called, *The Legend of Stumpie's Brae*. The first verse of which is in the grand old come-all-ye tradition:

> '*Heard ye no' tell of the Stumpie's brae?*
> *Sit down, sit down, young friend,*
> *I'll make your flesh to creep today*
> *And your hair to stan' on end.*'

Her toughness also showed in the ambitions she had for her husband. From the impoverished hills of Tyrone, he rose to become bishop of Derry, and eventually Primate, though the high office came to him four years after his wife's death. She was seventy-seven when she died on October 15th, 1895, in the Bishop's Palace in Derry, with William at her bedside. Today there are many memorials to her, including a window in St Columb's Cathedral, plaques in many other Ulster churches, and a row of alms houses near Bishop's Gate. But the most lasting memory will be the one which will be sung at Easter every year, '*There is a green hill far away, without a city wall, where the DEAR LORD was crucified, who died to save us all.*'

Chapter 13

The Question was Popped

It was a night in November 1962 that was to change my trajectory in life forever. My brothers and I had gone to a Young Farmers' dance in Cloughmills Orange Hall. The Dave Glover Showband was playing when Norman came up to me and asked me to dance. He was tall, although I couldn't say he was handsome, he had a discoloured tooth from a rugby injury, but he was a great mover on the dance floor. He had on a green tweed suit which he liked, and I detested. The Dave Glover Showband was one of the most popular bands of the sixties and their fan club followed them all over the country. I had a few dances with Norman, but when he asked to leave me home, I had someone else in my eye and opted for the other guy.

A couple of months later, Norman phoned to ask me to accompany him to Coleraine Rugby Club's formal dinner dance in Fawcett's Hotel Portrush. I was only sixteen and not very streetwise at that stage, and my parents initially wouldn't let me go. However, because my brothers knew Norman, they convinced them that I would be in safe hands. I bought a lovely peach dress in Paul Fashions, and white satin shoes, which I dyed to match the dress — you improvised in those days. I thought I was *'no goat's toe'* when I set off on my first date with Norman. However, there were constraints; I had to be home by a certain time.

Like Cadbury's old slogan about their Roses chocolates, '*They grow on you,*' likewise, Norman eventually grew on me, and we had an on-off relationship over five years until the night of the 20th of May 1967, when he proposed to me on the steps of Mainlea Guesthouse, Ballymena, a week before my 21st birthday. We organised an engagement/birthday party in the Lismara Hotel in Portrush. Unbeknown to me, in the time-honoured fashion, Norman had already asked my dad for my hand in marriage — apparently, they were leaning over a gate on our farm at the time.

We planned to build a house and get married in 1969, but Norman suggested we get married the next year (1968) and move in with his parents until our house was ready. July 26th was to be the big day. The wheels were set in motion. The Northern Counties Hotel in Portrush was the venue for the reception after the twelve-noon wedding ceremony in Aghadowey Presbyterian Church. The church was beautifully decorated by Miss Margaret Torrens with flowers from Greenmount Horticultural College, Antrim, where Margaret was employed. The splendid menu for the reception at the Counties comprised of a starter - vegetable broth and a roll, and the main course was roast beef with all the trimmings. There was Charlotte Russe for dessert, followed by wedding cake and coffee or tea.

The ceremony was performed by Dr J H Davey, our esteemed minister assisted by Dr T H Mullin, while Mrs Margaret McCloskey was the soloist. I carried a crescent bouquet of cream and pink orchids, stephanotis and lily of the valley. I wore a gown in iridescent white, which had an embroidered design in satin stitch and silver lurex. The gown was simply styled with a three-section skirt gathered at the back and the front, with a low-necked sleeveless bodice. Over that was a layer of white crystal satin with a matching plain white satin Eton jacket. The back panels of the jacket flowed into a full court train. My headdress of Swiss lace leaves, with rolled satin roses at the centre, was attached to a full-length veil edged with Swiss lace. Miss Eithne Cameron, a cousin, and Miss Norma Black, a friend, were bridesmaids. They wore gowns of satin *poult de soie* in goblin blue, with sleeveless, fitted bodices, slightly flared skirts that had inverted pleats down the centre front. The hems of the back-buttoned jackets were shorter at the front and curved lower at the back. The set-in sleeves were made of white Swiss guipure lace. They carried bouquets of white carnations. The child attendants were seven-year-old twins Joyce and Gladys McMichael, friends of the family. They were attired in gowns of white nylon *clair de lune*, simply styled with moulded tight-fitting bodices, puff sleeves and round necklines. Their headdresses were white bows and they carried pink floral balls. Cyril, the groom's friend, was best man and the groomsman was my brother Jack. Joseph (Joe) and my brother Mervyn were ushers. All the men were dressed in morning suits including my dad. Norman's dad being rather conservative chose to wear black jacket and striped trousers.

The summer of 1968 was a very dry sunny year. Norman rented twenty-five acres for hay on the Ballymoney line, where the Causeway Hospital now stands. Lots of naysayers said that he would never get the hay saved, but it was well saved, and all the bales were sold out of the fields as a cash crop. The sun shone for weeks, particularly on our wedding day, which allowed photos to be taken in Antrim Gardens across the road from the hotel. There were no evening parties in those days, so we set off on our honeymoon at 4:30 p.m., driven to a hotel in Belfast by our best man Cyril Millar. My *'going away'* outfit was a pink and turquoise dress and jacket with matching hat and navy accessories. Before our departure some rascals or so-called friends, *'kidnapped'* Norman, tied him on a trailer and gave him a fully-fledged tour of Portrush, while I was left to twiddle my thumbs until he returned, unscathed I may add.

The night preceding the wedding was frightening. Norman had come in the early evening to Knockaduff to pick up the flowers for the buttonholes. On his return home he saw William Cochrane sawing a large branch from a tree on which he was sitting. He was on the wrong side, and he fell to the ground. Meanwhile across the drive, William Taylor and a few mates had set fire to Frank Dinsmore's prized hay cocks in his cottage garden. As Norman proceeded further, a houseful of dry sows had been let loose and were enjoying their unexpected freedom to roam the farmyard. Aunty Jean heard the commotion and wisely rounded up all the young culprits and invited them in for a midnight feast. I think her lavish gesture embarrassed them and after enjoying her hospitality, they went home satisfied that they had completed their usual pre-wedding pranks successfully. When dawn broke in the morning, Nana, always well organised, had bathed and donned her elastic stockings and nylons in readiness for the wedding at noon. On discovering there were no buttonholes, she asked Norman if he had brought them, only to be told that they were in the back of the car. A thorough search took place, but to no avail, so Nana decided to mount her bicycle and search the driveway. Towards the far end she saw the missing buttonholes lying safely in a box in a trench. Horror of horrors, on her return to the house, she discovered her stockings had come in contact with grease from the bicycle chain.

Nana Ruby always liked clothes on the *'clever'* side, which meant they were always on the big side. When Norman put on his wedding shirt, he found it had a sixteen-inch collar instead of fifteen. Aunty Jean came to his aid once again and rushed into town and returned with the proper size. There were no more episodes, and it was a memorable day all round.

After staying in Belfast, we took the train to Dublin to catch a flight to Ibiza for a two-week stay. The Hotel Tagomago was on San Antonio Bay and was much less commercialised then, as was the whole island. There were old, black-clothed women picking almonds at the back of our hotel. There were no nudist beaches there at that time, until I broke with tradition. We were on an inflatable when I slipped off. When I clambered back on board, I had lost my bikini top. Norman plunged into the sea, recovered it and stopped it from floating away.

Post was much more reliable in those days, and we received a letter from my mum which gave us an update on what was happening at home. There was still no rain after six weeks. But two days after our return, it arrived.

In those days, it was the custom to show off the wedding presents and Mum had done just that, as she entertained folk every night with her legendary sponge cakes and so forth. We returned on a Sunday from our honeymoon, and as no liaising took place, dinner was prepared by both households. I don't remember which one we chose. Then it was back to the grind of farming while I continued to travel to work in Ballymena until our home was ready. Being newly married, it wasn't unusual to have the odd lie in and on one such morning Norman's dad shouted up the stairs, *"Are you going to lie up there all day?"*

CHAPTER 14

Establishing a Home

Norman and I returned after a lovely two-week honeymoon in Ibiza to a new life as a married couple. I continued working in Ballymena and helped on the farm at weekends, and every Sunday morning I cooked an Ulster fry. The contractor Howard Platt, who would build our new home gave us the middle price of £7,500 for a four-bedroom house on a green field site on the farm. It was good to live close to the building project and liaise with the builder at every stage of the work. Our good friend Sammy Richmond completed a well-equipped kitchen and washroom for £250. Auntie Jean bought us a dishwasher, with a cold-water fill, which was very unusual in that era. She was still under the Canadian influence, after spending some years in Toronto.

In February 1970, the house was ready for occupancy. In the sixties you just furnished a room as you went along. I remember potatoes were a good price and the revenue from their sale almost paid for the construction of our house. No mortgage was taken out and we paid the builder over the two-year period, while it was being built.

The house- warming took place and as people gathered, Auntie Jean broke a Parker Knoll sofa as she plumped herself down. Luckily, it was replaced by the reputable firm of McConkey and Gould, Coleraine.

I joined Ballyrashane Presbyterian Church[18] at the time of my marriage. The Ballyrashane Parish was founded in 1657, and for the centenary year, a new roof was put on the present church building. At that time many members of the church purchased a square of linen for half a crown (25p). The donor's family name was embroidered on it and each square was sown together to make a large quilt. This was an ingenious way of contributing to the new roof project. The quilt is on display in the link between the church and the hall.

The first minister of Ballyrashane was a Scotsman, the Reverend Robert Hogsyard. According to records at Glasgow University, he was the son of Robert Hogsyard, a citizen of Glasgow, and he obtained his MA in 1655. After a period of reluctance to respond to the call of God and move to Ireland, he arrived in March 1657. He was ordained at the presbytery meeting on November 5th of that year. In the transcripts, he is recorded as receiving £100 per year from the Commonwealth from September 29, 1657. However, in 1600 King Charles II was restored to the English throne. Very soon after, episcopy was re-established in Ireland and all ministers were required either to resign from their churches or conform to prelacy. The Reverend Robert Hogsyard refused to comply with this request and continued serving his church. Having ignored a second written request, a large troop of Dragoons arrived to arrest him while he was preaching in his church in 1661. It is recorded that Hogsyard showed no fear and asked that he might finish his sermon before leaving his church and ministry. Following his ejection, he remained, like many other ministers of his day, among his people for a time, preaching until it was physically impossible for him to continue. In 1663, he was confined with nine other ministers to two private houses in Carrickfergus, under house arrest. A few weeks later, the ministers were given the choice of being sent to the West of Ireland or of leaving the country. Mr Hogsyard chose to leave Ireland. He died prior to January 1673, and left two sons Robert and Thomas, who were minors.

---

[18] See page 225 - Endnote

Today, we take our religious freedom for granted, as well as the sacrifices our forefathers made for our religious liberty. After the ejection of their minister, the congregation at Ballyrashane built a sod church at Knockinkeeragh but later moved to a site behind Brookhall, which was called *Nancy's Knowe*. There they built a thatched church with lead windows, an earthen floor and fir blocks from the bog for seats. There have been fourteen ministers since the Rev Hogsyard was installed in 1657. There were no cushioned pews in those days.

In the sixties, farming was very different from today, as we say, *'eggs weren't kept in the one basket,'* so there were many enterprises carried out, dairying, pig rearing, sheep, poultry, barley and potatoes. Nowadays, it is more specialised and streamlined. Haymaking gave way to the *crazy* idea of silage making. At Tullans potato growing was the main enterprise and it brought much excitement when a potato harvester replaced the spinner. Only four helpers were necessary and again the local women were employed. One famous woman called Margaret comes to mind. In the spring the crop was planted by two people who were seated on either side of a large bin of potatoes which were dropped down a shute into the drill. A bell rang each time one was dropped. Our minister's wife Pat Connor filled the breach one day when we were short-staffed. Later she told us that she was hearing bells in her sleep.

The aforementioned, Margaret, was the kind of character that you would never forget. She had a pronounced squint in her left eye and a foul mouth. She didn't suffer fools gladly and was famous for her excessive indulgence of alcohol at weekends. I will never forget my first encounter with her, and her loud and lewd language. However, because of her diligent work ethic, Norman was happy to forgo her complex nature.

Margaret was full of stories. She told us about one Twelfth Night, in Bertie Peacock's bar in Long Commons, Coleraine. It was a busy night and, as there was no taxi available or a lift home with Bertie Peacock, the proprietor. Margaret set out alone for her home at *Windyhall*, two miles away. She had proceeded a short distance along Beresford Road when she fell into a hole in the hedge. She was woken on Sunday morning by the peal of the chapel bells. After dusting herself down, the brave Margaret headed the two miles home. On arrival, she realised her dentures were missing and her husband Campbell was sent in search of the prodigal choppers. Her husband went straight to the spot and sure enough the dentures were sitting undisturbed in the hole in the hedge opposite St Malachy's Chapel.

On another occasion I was taking tea to the potato field when I saw Margaret waving frantically. As I got closer, she spoke. *"The oul woman has fell aff at the bottom o' the field and that Norman boy hasn't missed her,"* she said. Nana, who was eighty plus, and on the harvester, but was superfluous to needs, as there were already four people on it. Norman had removed the safety bar to accommodate her. As he turned the corner at speed, sure enough, Nana was thrown to the ground in a heap, thankfully unhurt. All these episodes added a tad of lustre to the potato harvesting.

I always fancied a Jersey cow, so Lisa was purchased from a neighbour Ian Dalzell. Everyone but me enjoyed the creamy milk she produced. She won her class at Coleraine Show and was greatly admired. However, the novelty wore off, as no one wanted to relieve me of my milking duties morning and night, and eventually she was sold back to her former owner.

Cows are quite similar to goats in many ways, in that they have their own characteristics. The story is told of a minister who had a goat to provide milk for the manse. The family went on holiday and the maid was left to milk the goat, only to find that she would not let down the milk for a stranger. Not to be defeated, the maid went into the manse, donned the minister's vestments and without a word spoken, sat down on a stool and a bucket of milk was forthcoming.

The AGA cooker was still in place in the farmhouse when Auntie Jean, Nana's sister, came to live there. She wanted an open fire and persuaded Nana to take out the AGA and replace it with a Devon Grate. It was something Nana always regretted. The exceedingly heavy cooker was taken from pillar to post, and I eventually advertised it for sale in the local paper, but it was to no avail. When a new cattle house was erected, the space around the slurry tank needed filling, so the redundant AGA was broken up and used in a different way - what a waste.

An old disused house on the farm had an ancient black range made by H&T Bellas and called *The Bann Range*. I painlessly disassembled it bit by bit into probably about twenty pieces before I laid them out carefully so Norman could bring them to the farm. He arrived with the link box for transporting farm tools attached to the tractor and we carefully loaded our precious antique. He was driving a little too fast for comfort when he hit a stone and dropped the link-box. The rest is history! I called a local engineer to survey the damage, only to be told the range was cast iron and couldn't be welded and so it was beyond repair.

The link box played a significant part on one other day. There were two elderly bachelors, Davy and Jim who lived in Mayrs's house up our back lane. Davy was a tall man with broad shoulders, and he was rather shy. Jim was the opposite, small in stature, very chatty but quick tempered. They didn't get along as brothers and so they lived at separate ends of their house. They had a primitive existence, with no running water, so they fetched all their water from a well halfway up the lane. Both were civil men, and Davy was known as one of the best drain diggers in the locality. He dug every drain with a spade and shovel. Sadly, he lost the sight in one eye while digging near a thorn hedge. A branch penetrated his eye and did irreparable damage.

On one occasion I had to call a GP for Jim. Dr Fitzimmons duly arrived but couldn't approach the house by car. I took the doctor, case and all on the link box for the journey of about 800 yards. She was highly amused and said she would insert this experience in the *Medical Journal* as a mode of transport for a patient in the seventies.

Jim was eccentric and often called at our house often for tea and soda bread. One night, Jim called to say he wasn't too well, yet he was still smoking his pipe, and leaving a semicircle of dead matches around his feet on the kitchen floor. Again, I called the doctor. Dr McMaster duly arrived and examined the patient, only to be told by Jim that he wanted to stay with Mrs McClelland for the night. The doctor reasoned with him and said that I had a young family to attend to and hadn't room. Eventually an ambulance was called, and Jim was taken to a psychiatric facility at Gransha Hospital, Londonderry. On another occasion David came to tell us that he thought Jim was, *"lying dead up there."* Sadly, Jim had passed away and a glass of milk was lying by his bedside.

Frank and Cissy Dinsmore were great neighbours who lived at the end of our drive. Cissy was a seamstress and Frank was a cooper, as was his father. He was a tall, fine-looking man with a distinctive Donegal brogue and a great shock of grey hair. He had a fantastic memory and was a great raconteur, who gave recitations at church socials. Sometimes he had to be encouraged to leave the platform and return to his seat. He often hitched a lift by waving a white hanky, and sometimes caused motorists to swerve to avoid him. He came from Stranorlar in Donegal and Cissy came from Strabane. Frank was a wonderful craftsman, and I was fascinated to see how he made watertight barrels without using any nails. Traditionally, a cooper made wooden casks, tubs and troughs from timber staves, held together with metal hoops. The wood was made pliable by steeping it in water. Frank made me a lovely wooden log tub many years ago. When it dries out and the staves become loose, I leave it outside in the rain to expand the staves again.

Frank's tiny workshop was full of treasured tools, many belonging to his late father. Frank was a good all–rounder when it came to fixing anything from shafting a spade to patching a bucket. He was almost indispensable around our farm. Both Frank and Cissy are still greatly missed at Tullans. Cissy used to say, *"If the Lord calls me I'll say I can't go, I have to babysit up at McClelland's."* Frank used to repair barrels for Bushmills Distillery, sampling the dregs from the barrels for merriment. He went to Armagh to stay for some time each summer to carry out repair work in a jam factory. He had a wonderful repertoire of poems, and he gave me one in 1980. Apparently, his inspiration came during the reign of King George V,

> *'I William the Norman*
> *Then William his son*
> *Henry, Steven, Richard and John (signed the Magna Carta 1215)*
> *Queen Anne, the Georges*
> *And William's Reign's done!*
> *And then Queen Victoria and Seventh Edward*
> *And George V his son.'*

When I was in Strabane, Norman gave the couple a lift to visit friends and he also said Frank's recitations kept him from sleeping at the wheel.

CHAPTER 15

Time for Family

I had resigned from my job at O'Kane's in Ballymena and enjoyed setting up our new home in 1971. It was a year of changes and a turbulent year again in Northern Ireland politics. The Prime Minister, James Chichester-Clark met with the British prime minister to discuss the security situation in Northern Ireland.

Other events that happened that year included the following:

• *The first Women's Liberation march took place in London.*

• *Winnie Mandela, anti-apartheid activist and politician was sentenced to a one-year jail term.*

• *It was billed the 'fight of the century,' when Muhammad Ali, took on Joe Frazier, the man who had taken his title, at Madison Square Garden in New York on March 7, 1971. Ali had been stripped of his World Heavyweight Championship title and suspended from boxing for three years after refusing to fight in the Vietnam War.*

• *Three members of the Royal Highland Fusiliers were killed by members of the IRA. Four thousand shipyard workers took to the streets to demand internment because of the slaughter.*

- *Later that year, Brian Faulkner became prime minister of Northern Ireland when he succeeded James Chichester-Clark.*

- *A stairway crush at a Rangers versus Celtic football match caused the death of sixty people.*

- *Education Secretary, Margaret Thatcher, who later became Prime Minister, ended free school milk for children over the age of seven.*

- *The microprocessor was invented, perhaps marking the start of the digital age. There was a greater use of transistor technology, for example in things like hand-held calculators, originally very expensive.*

- *It was also the first year North Sea oil production began in Norway.*

- *Another major transition was the change to decimal currency in the UK and Ireland.*

- *BBC Open University began this year in the UK.*

- *Rolls-Royce went bankrupt and was nationalised.*

- *The postal workers' strike ended after forty-seven days. Things never change over the course of time for some people.*

- *Evel Knievel, an American daredevil, set a world record by jumping over nineteen cars on his motorbike. And you think Joey Dunlop was a genius!*

- *Mount Etna in Sicily erupted again and threatened several small villages on the eastern side of the volcano.*[19]

---

[19] Adapted from https://www.thepeoplehistory.com/1971.html

Yes, 1971 was a year of changes, but the greatest change for us, was the arrival of a baby at Tullans. We were settling into our new abode, but the tranquil ambience around us was about to change. I had an appointment with my GP and on my arrival home I said to Norman, *"That wee test proved positive."* We were both delighted and a new experience of parenthood had started.

On the morning of March 26th, 1971, the day was different. Mild contractions were coming at a slow pace, and I was cleaning the silver when Mum, not knowing about my pain, phoned to hear how I was. Norman had invited a friend in to see our house and have tea - a prolonged visit. By the evening I was ready for the short journey across the river to the Mary Ranken Maternity Hospital. After being ten days overdue David Joseph arrived at 8:40 p.m. and weighed 8lbs 9ozs. He had a ginger streak down the centre of a mop of golden curly hair.

I wasn't used to babies and was very inexperienced, but I soon got to know the ropes as a young mother. We had plenty of babysitting offers from Nana and Mrs Dinsmore at the end of the drive. David became so used to having adults around him, he was quite advanced in his speech. On one occasion when I took him to the GP, he asked him to lift his wing (arm) to check his temperature. David looked up at me and in his childish talk. *"I no' like that man,"* he said. I booked him into playschool and when our minister called, he asked David where it was. He replied in a very polite voice, *"I think it's in England, sir."*

CHAPTER 16

The Day Our Baby Died

Time and tide wait for no man; I became pregnant again when David was a year old. My pregnancy went well, and I was as fit as a fiddle. November 15th, 1972, changed everything. Someone came for potatoes, but there were no men around to help load them. As the man was on his own, I suggested I would haul the bags across the store floor and not lift them, just to help. Later that evening, I had little twinges of pain, not dissimilar to contractions and realised something wasn't quite right. We headed to Route Hospital where I was admitted, and it was confirmed that I was in labour. After some difficult hours a baby boy was delivered into my welcoming arms. Sadly, he only survived three hours. I was devastated. Norman was heartbroken too, but we supported each other and with our compassionate minister we arranged the funeral. I so wanted to see my little one's remains being lowered into the ground in Coleraine Cemetery, but it wasn't possible as I was still in hospital. Some fifty years ago women didn't attend funerals. There were only four in attendance, Reverend Mullin, Norman, and the two grandpas — my dad and Norman's dad.

I vividly recall sobbing my heart out in that private ward at one o'clock, the time of the funeral. There wasn't a nurse or anyone to comfort me in my loss. Nowadays, there would be counselling support and full back-up help. However, although I wasn't a Christian at the time, I knew that our little one had gone to Heaven and I derived much comfort from that fact. When I went to my GP, Dr McMaster Senior, for my postnatal consultation he was very helpful. He said our wee baby had seemed perfectly healthy, but only God knows the reason why he died. He said he knew a little boy in Coleraine who had been born blind. He explained that too much oxygen can cause blindness and too little causes brain damage, and that there was a very fine line between the two. He was my counsellor. In those days they weren't so far advanced in neonatology as they are today. I don't dwell on it, but I sometimes wonder if it may have been the potato handling that caused the premature birth. Life began to have some sort of semblance of normality again, and being busy with a toddler did help enormously.

In the summer of 1973, I was pregnant again and keeping well. The baby was due on January the 1st, 1974. We were invited to a friend's house for New Year's Eve, so we went with my case in the boot. Three days later, on January the 3rd, 1974, Ian, a bouncing baby boy, was born. He had a lot of blonde spiky hair, a broad face and weighed 8lbs 6ozs. Before I was due for discharge, I noticed the baby twitching slightly, but none of the staff saw it. However, on our arrival home, I was still concerned and called our GP Dr Fitzimons late that night. Baby Ian didn't oblige to twitch, but the doctor stayed for a lengthy period and suggested I bath the baby. Shortly after I put him in the bath, it became obvious that there was a problem, and my anxiety was justified. Because it was late on a Saturday night and *The Troubles* were causing problems around the Royal Victoria Hospital, she suggested we should take him into Coleraine Hospital instead. I stayed most of the night and returned home in the morning. I wasn't long home when a paramedic came to our house to say our baby's condition had worsened. Our phone was out of order, hence the visit by the hospital staff. At the hospital we were ushered into a ward where our very sick baby was in an oxygen tent.

I immediately asked for an appointment with a paediatrician, who then decided Ian should be transferred to the Royal Victoria Hospital for sick children. Early on the Monday morning I was in an ambulance along with a nurse who was given the task of monitoring the frequency of the twitches. It seemed a long fifty-five-mile journey in the ambulance, especially when the nurse informed me our baby was twitching every four minutes. A nursing sister was awaiting our arrival, and we were soon taken to a ward with lots of crying babies. I tried to compose myself, but naturally I was tearful when the nurse put her arm around my shoulder and took me across the ward to four cots. *"Mrs McClelland, don't worry, those four babies have the same condition and are all on the road to recovery,"* she said. That was Monday. On Tuesday they gave him calcium intravenously, then his calcium levels began to rise upwards. By Thursday we brought Ian back to Tullans.

Before our first baby was born, I approached my doctor about breast-feeding. He was adamant that as a farmer's wife I wouldn't have the time. *"Don't be coming to me with breast blisters,"* he said. So, on his advice I didn't get to carry out my wish. That was an era when breast-feeding was taboo and not at all in vogue. Because I didn't feed David, I felt I couldn't breastfeed baby Ian, so that was where the problem began. Unlike his older brother, who was a very slow feeder, always falling asleep on the bottle, baby Ian gulped it down in record time and was still hungry. The health visitor suggested changing from *SMA*, a milder fortified milk, to *Cow and Gate*, a more substantial milk. Because of the speed at which he drank it, his body couldn't absorb sufficient calcium into his bloodstream, which resulted in muscle spasms and a condition called hypocalcaemia. Medics today say the best source of calcium is obtained from the mother's milk.

Irene was my second cousin who was our faithful babysitter and looked after David and baby Ian during the funeral of Grandpa McClelland, who passed away on 27th January 1974 just a few weeks after Ian's birth. When I arrived back at the house to see how things were going, Irene had enthusiastically administered gripe water and the stench of it met me at the door. But it did the trick and Irene was employed on many occasions for years.

Thankfully, as for Ian, he had no ill effects from his illness: he participated in football and rugby for many years, is now nearly fifty and still coaching young lads coming through Coleraine Rugby Football Club; as well as being a busy farmer and proprietor of a caravan park on the farm.

CHAPTER 17

When Royalty Arrives

The sun was shining on a Thursday afternoon in August 1977, when Queen Elizabeth and the Duke of Edinburgh arrived for a garden party in their Wessex Helicopter, just six minutes behind schedule, at the New University of Ulster, Coleraine Campus. Hearts and flowers awaited them on their tour of the university. The couple stopped to admire the Jubilee cake which had been baked by a Macosquin woman, Mrs Jean Craig. The cake, baked in a heart shape, was a pink and white confection, decorated with fondant icing and bore the figure twenty-five in appropriate royal icing. It won first prize in a competition run by the Northern Ireland Women's Institute. Mrs Craig, a keen member of the WI, and her daughter Marie were presented to the Queen. Not only did Mrs Craig bake the royal cake, but she was responsible for the flower arrangements in The Diamond at the New University of Ulster Coleraine.

There was no stone left unturned, with stringent measures in place across the 300-acre site. Earlier in the day a gun and a quantity of ammunition were discovered in a quarry at Danes Hill, near the University. The discovery was made at 11:05 a.m. by the Security Forces. Another little incident that largely went unnoticed took place during the afternoon's proceedings. A light aircraft appeared, flying over the campus. All private flying was banned, and an army helicopter quickly diverted the offending aircraft. Mr Wheeler, chairman of Moyle District Council chatted to the Duke. *"He asked*

*me my occupation and I told him I was an architect. The Duke smiled
and wondered if I had anything to do with the design of this place?"* [20]
Alderman John White was the mayor of Coleraine at the time of the
visit and told the story of Queen Elizabeth sitting beside him at the
banquet table. On discovering a little rag nail and not being able to
chew it because the cameras were on her, she quipped to John, *"It can
be a nasty little thing, can't it?*

The seventeen-year-old Prince Andrew had young female hearts
fluttering when he unexpectedly joined his mother and father for the
afternoon youth festival at the University. The prince was making his
first ever appearance in Northern Ireland and the announcement made
just after lunch, that he would attend the festival, was greeted with loud
screams and enthusiastic applause, especially from the young women.
His visit gave local girls the opportunity to see their royal idol in the
flesh and he was met everywhere with loud chants of, *"Andrew! Andrew!"*
as he toured many stands and enjoyed the afternoon's activities. Prince
Andrew, with his warm smile, good looks and friendly personality, was
the centre of attention of all the young folk, despite only staying an
hour and a half and not attending the garden party. He certainly scored
a hit with the Ulster girls and was given a tremendous send off as he left
by helicopter to return to the royal yacht.

When local women were asked about the colour of Queen Elizabeth's
ensemble, they said it was sky-blue or powder blue. It was neither.
The striking royal figure was in periwinkle-blue and white, echoing
the colour of the Mediterranean-like skies over the University. It was a
slim-fitting dress and jacket in silk and the full-skirted dress fell in soft
pleats. Her hat was blue straw with a crown of small white silk flowers.
Neat white court shoes, white gloves and white bag completed the
pretty summery outfit.

---

[20] Taken from Coleraine Chronicle archives.

On Thursday evening, thousands paid a shoreline homage and gave *Britannia* a huge send-off from Portrush. Only the privileged who had been invited saw the sovereign at close range during her stay in Northern Ireland. But that didn't stop thousands giving her a coastal salute. It was a warm August night that became the ultimate stage for the Queen's Jubilee Commonwealth tour. Rest and relaxation amid the quiet splendour of the western isles of Scotland lay ahead as the Royal Yacht Britannia upped anchor and glided away from the sweeping West Bay Portrush at the end of 40,000 miles of Jubilee touring of the seas.

I wonder if Her Majesty was moved by the Portrush Bon Voyage as the sun went down. Thousands of her subjects had come from near and far to gather under the bunting, just to see the 412–foot long royal yacht. They had been going to the shoreline all day, of course, to greet Britannia. But, when the pomp and ceremony was nearly over, and the queen was aboard and would be imminently sailing into the sultry night, magic was still in the air. There was no doubt that Britannia was a magnificent sight. To see it, savour it, imprint it indelibly on your mind, was the conscious intention of everyone there. Ramore Head, the harbour walls, the front of Barry's Amusements, the west-strand car park and up and beyond in Portstewart direction was *'black with people,'* as they say around here. They watched until *Britannia*, with a twenty-one-knot cruising speed, was a twinkling dot far out at sea.

The Royal Yacht *Britannia* was in service from 1954 to 1997. It is now retired from royal service, and permanently berthed at Ocean Terminal, Leith in Edinburgh. It is a major tourist attraction, with over 300,000 visits each year. Britannia was the eighty-third royal vessel since Charles II and during her forty-three-year career she travelled more than one million miles around the world to more than 600 ports in 135 countries.[21] I recommend a visit, but advance booking is essential.

---

[21] https://en.wikipedia.org/wiki/HMY_Britannia

CHAPTER 18

Green, Green Grass of Home

Although farming was a busy all year-round profession, we always arranged an annual family holiday. Our family had increased to four. Ross arrived bang on time on his due date March 16, 1976, weighing 7lbs 8ozs, and is still a good timekeeper. He also had a head of blonde hair and very fine features. In fact, Aunty Jean quipped, *"Wouldn't he make a lovely wee girl?"* My GP decided to induce me as she was going on holiday the next day. The senior GP visited me after a difficult birth and said, *"Sometimes it's best to let nature take its course."* Enough said.

Ruth arrived four days late, on June the 5, 1978, and weighed 7lbs 7ozs. She had brown hair and a lovely round face. I was so surprised that it was a girl that I asked the midwife 'if she was sure.' Then along came a proud dad with a bunch of red roses and a card that said, *'Didn't we do well?'* A parking ticket was on the windscreen when he returned to the car, bringing him back to earth.

Holiday packing for six was down to a fine art and great experiences were written in the annals for the future. Donegal was nearer to home, and we loved that destination. Crossing the border caused my adrenalin to pump as if we were in a foreign land. I recall one such holiday when the Adams's asked us to go to a caravan at Marble Hill, County Donegal. I had noticed an Irish Wolfhound wandering around the park. Norman wasn't enamoured as he had to carry water from a distance and take a cold shower. When he returned to the caravan with the water, taking his first step up to the van, a dog nipped his heel. By the sound of him I thought it was the hound, but it turned out to be a wee Jack Russell Terrier. I think its bark was worse than its bite. Little did we know that this one and only caravan experience would lead to hundreds of caravans descending on our farm more than fifty years later.

The Royal Show in Stoneleigh Warwickshire was an amazing Agricultural Show, although it no longer exists. We stayed in the beautiful Cotswolds on our way home and stopped at Stratford-Upon-Avon to enjoy a cruise on the Avon. Of course, Avon is famous for being the birthplace of William Shakespeare, known as the Bard of Avon and the greatest playwright and dramatist of all time. Shakespeare married Ann Hathaway, eight years his senior, when he was eighteen, according to the inscription on their gravestone. There were 'toy boys' in those days too! They had three children, Susanna and twins Judith and Hammet, sadly Hammet died at age eleven. There is some dispute about how many plays Shakespeare wrote, but the general consensus is thirty-seven. One of his famous sayings is, *'A fool thinks himself to be wise, but a wise man knows himself to be a fool.'* Another equally famous quote is, *'Love all, trust a few, do wrong to none.'* His most famous plays include Hamlet (1600); Macbeth (1605); Midsummer Night's Dream (1595); The Merchant of Venice (1596); Romeo and Juliet (1594); Twelfth Night (1599); Henry IV, Henry V, Henry VI. And Henry VIII.

The Isle of Man was a favourite destination holiday before continental holidays came into vogue. The first time we went there was in 1979, with the Richmond family, six years after the disastrous Summerland fire on August the 2nd, 1973, when fifty people, including eleven children perished and eighty more were injured. Summerland was the largest holiday complex in Europe and sadly the tragedy was caused by three boys smoking in a disused kiosk. However, we had a memorable week on the island, riding on the tram and cycling on tandem bikes. The highlight was a women's wrestling match. I got rather carried away when the underdog was getting a battering, and I had to be restrained from exiting my ringside seat to thump the assailant with my handbag! We stayed in a B&B on the promenade. Full board for a week, two adults and three children, came to £20.50. The children were intrigued with the manual lift that conveyed food from the kitchen below to the dining room above. We had a problem keeping the children from trying to operate the rope on this strange contraption. Sammy, our friend, fancied himself as a commodore, so we hired a boat and had a few nerve-wracking incidents when, instead of lifting his foot off the pedal, he increased the throttle as he negotiated the corners of the lake. When Norman produced a £100 note, Sammy's eyes nearly popped out, he'd never seen one before. That was when spuds were a good trade.

In the 80's we enjoyed many holidays in Jersey, Majorca and Malta with the Henry family. But it would be a trip to the Winter Fair in London that'll never be forgotten.

It was December, with frost on the ground. When we were passing Ballymena on our way to the International Airport, I discovered I had left the tickets in the writing desk at Tullans. After breaking all speed restrictions, the tickets were recovered, and we boarded the plane by the skin of our teeth. As I said there was a severe frost and Norman kept phoning home on a regular basis to check that the heaters were on so that the potatoes were kept frost free. Because of fog and frost our return flight was cancelled and the alternative route was by coach to Stranraer Ferry. We were well on our way to Victoria Coach Station when my brother Ivor, (he and his wife were with us) announced that he had left his shoes under the bed. I said forget about them. But he said he couldn't, because they belonged to his dad. Fortunately, we recovered the shoes in time to catch the coach to Scotland. There was no 'third' episode, and we returned home safely, and the potatoes were fine.

We booked a coach holiday to Austria, not realising it would take almost three days travel to get there, and the same coming back home, which left us just five days to enjoy our beautiful destination. However, there is always a character or two on any coach trip we've been on and certainly this one didn't disappoint. Her name was Lily, she came from Bangor and had just buried her third husband. She was a laugh a minute, aged around eighty, with peroxide bleached hair in a French roll, and she had a very quick wit. After dinner there was a singsong with the German tourists joining in. They had become louder than the Irish crowd, when Lily jumped on the table, and shook her fist. *"Well, we won the war anyway,"* she shouted.

I entered the *Belfast Newsletter* competition to win a three-day mini cruise to France with Irish Ferries — and I won. It was a wet October day when we headed off, with our good friends Sammy and Margaret Richmond, to Rosslare. We stayed in a lovely B&B enroute and, of course, Sammy never liked to by-pass an antique shop in search of a bargain, however the table he took a liking to was too big for the boot. All went well, but unfortunately our berth was directly above the engine room and my head started to pound because of the noise from the engine. We were to have a meal when the vessel sailed, but all I wanted to do was put my head down and forgo the food. On arrival in Zeebrugge, I was glad to get to land. We spent a super day of retail therapy, and I didn't board the ferry without my Sea Legs medication so I could enjoy a good night's sleep.

One year, we travelled to Vichy in the Auvergne-Rhône-Alpes region of France as guests of the Charolais Cattle Club. It was a learning curve for all of us as we weren't very fluent in French, but we soon learnt to ask for steaks, *'bien cuit'* (well done). When the steaks were first presented to us very rare, Norman didn't like the look of them, especially when he noticed several French men biting into the meat, blood dripping down their chins. However, over the years, he learnt to appreciate a steak cooked medium to rare.

We enjoyed a family holiday in Jersey and visited the war tunnels, an underground German hospital, and a chilling reminder of World War II. This war has become something that seems to belong to the previous century. For most visitors to Jersey those years of global conflict are a very distant memory or just pages in a history book. Nevertheless, for the people of Jersey, the Second World War was a unique and harrowing experience. For five long years the Channel Islands were occupied by German forces. They are the only British soil that was invaded and occupied. The forces that occupied Jersey in the 1940s left an indelible mark, not only on the history of the island, but also on the landscape. The most fascinating feature is the vast underground hospital created by the occupiers when Allied invasion was imminent. It takes just a few steps into the German underground hospital to realise what a feat of engineering was achieved by forced labour from every corner of conquered Europe. It is no fun theme park, rather it is the real thing, hewn in human history. Our boys, even at a young age were fascinated by it, so much so that when I went to check on Ian in our bedroom, he was sitting up on the bed and had just painted a swastika on his chest with my red nail polish. That was the same polish that David said he didn't like as I looked like a *bad woman* when I put it on. Jersey always appealed to us as the currency was the same as ours and you didn't need a passport to travel there.

It was July 1987, when we were invited to Tracey McIntyre's wedding in London, Ontario, Canada. Tracey's parents Gilmour (Gil) and Norma had been bequeathed a farm in the beautiful spot called Whitepark Bay on the north coast of Northern Ireland. They were related to Norman's mum and had never been to Ireland, but on their first visit they immediately fell in love with the place and have returned many times since to breathe the North Antrim air and enjoy the picturesque landscape. Tracey's sister Gayle has a soft spot for the place and says she could happily live here. They were enthralled when they visited the Giant's Causeway, and Carrick-a-Rede rope bridge and viewed the remote old farmstead where they recovered a rather battered stone dog ornament, which now adorns their home in

Canada. It was a bitter-sweet experience as they recalled Tracey and Gayle's grandmother and twin sister leaving these shores when they were in their teens. There were no luxuries in those days, and they had very few worldly possessions when they set off for the land of opportunity. Both women found partners who had emigrated from Northern Ireland and once they were married, the two couples set up a home together. They used the large house to accommodate expatriates from Ireland who were in search of work. They produced a son each and decided they needed to separate, so they bought two properties only to find that the twin bond couldn't be broken. After some time, the couples were back together again, until they were separated by death. Their grandma McIntyre decided to go back to visit her mother in Ireland, leaving behind her husband and son. World War II broke out during her stay, and she couldn't return home for nearly two years. There was no way to correspond, so her husband didn't know whether his loved one was dead or alive.

Tracey's wedding was a grand affair and so different from back home. Her little nephew, Jamie, who was four, was pageboy. I admired his white silk suit. *"It's just hired,"* he said. The wedding took place in Oakridge Presbyterian Church London, Ontario, and the lavish reception was held at a golf club where Norman gave a speech on behalf of the Irish relatives. At the end of each speech a guest at that table would tinkle a glass and the people at that table broke into song. That tradition was new to us, and we were enjoying the music and dancing when a tape of Tom Jones singing *Green Green Grass of Home* was played. Suddenly, I felt a lump in my throat and managed to suppress the tears which weren't far away, as my mind turned to our four wee ones at home under the care of Nana and her cousin Lizzie May McVicker. The McIntyres have returned to Whitepark Bay many times and we've enjoyed hosting them at Tullans.

We had three weeks to spend there, so the week preceding the wedding we spent with the McIntyres. The middle week we went south by Greyhound Coach to visit the Hilsts in Havana, Illinois. Detroit was where we joined the coach for Illinois. It was scary, as we had never seen beggar women before, asking for *'a cent for a sausage.'* I had to pay a visit to the washroom and asked Norman to wait outside. When I came out, Norman had disappeared. I found him around the corner out of sight. He had noticed a sign, which was oblivious to me, and which was well displayed above the toilet door — *'No loitering around these toilets.'* He always had a lot of wisdom.

We arrived in Havana to a warm 111° F (44° C) welcome. Norman's mum had hosted Judy, a delegate representing the International Farm Youth Exchange (IFYE) in America. Norman was not great at correspondence, so his mum filled the breach until we married and then I took over the letter writing. Judy, her husband and three children came to visit us for their 25th wedding anniversary and so the friendship continued, with them returning to Ireland a few more times.

When the children were young, we had many day trips: Giant's Causeway, the steam train at Antrim Castle, Roe Valley Country Park, the Highland Show and the Dublin Show. We joined some of our church family to go to Rathlin Island on a beautiful summer's day. We had a picnic and saw the island at its best. On returning home I asked Norman if he'd enjoyed it. He said he enjoyed the food, but he wouldn't be rushing back. *"You'd see as much up our back lane as you'd see on Rathlin"* he quipped. I returned many times, but Norman kept to his word and never went back to Rathlin.

One summer, David, who lived in Aberdeenshire, asked us if we would like to join him at Campbeltown Show in Kintyre. As usual there were too many farm duties to complete, so Norman declined. I headed for Ballycastle to take the trip on a small boat which took only twelve passengers. I was never a good sailor and so when I was issued with a life jacket, it did nothing to quell my fears. However, I was seated at the back beside a Royal National Lifeboat Institution (RNLI) staff member The wee boat just seemed to be skimming the surface as we navigated Fair Head and went straight across to Kintyre. I shared my fear with him and asked what speed the skipper was doing. He assured me the sea was like a mill pond. The normal speed was usually twenty-five knots, but he thought we might be doing forty, so we should arrive in record time. After spending a few days with David and his family up in Aberdeenshire, I decided to take the conventional ferry for my return journey.

In 2009, we accompanied our daughter Ruth and her husband to Harrogate to the Ice Cream Alliance Competition where she won a silver award for her vanilla ice cream. They say that Harrogate is the jewel in North Yorkshire. The spa waters there contain iron sulphur and common salt and were discovered in the sixteenth century. There are many fine examples of architecture, and the Royal Hall was reopened by Prince Charles in 2008, following an eight-million-pound refurbishment. Betty's Café Tea Rooms is a must while visiting Harrogate. The variety of teas on offer was amazing, with Darjeeling being the champagne of teas. The luxury afternoon tea was a singularly stylish and devilish experience in opulent, elegant surroundings. The staff were extremely polite and wore black and white frilly aprons and white caps. Mobile phones were not allowed on the premises.

We returned to Canada for a third time, and this was to top all our former trips. Our family had kindly organised a visit to the Royal Agricultural Winter Fair in Toronto for Norman's 65th Birthday. In the Robert Pearson Airport, Toronto, everyone stood still to observe a minute's silence as it was Armistice Day and the 11th hour on the 11th of November 2003. It was a poignant moment to experience the business of an international airport come to a standstill to remember the victims of two World Wars.

The fair was an unforgettable experience. There were a myriad of stands relating to everything rural, from gigantic pumpkins of all shapes, colours and sizes to gardening requisites. Then there was the horse show at night which included carriage racing with the drivers holding on for grim death as the horses manoeuvred the corners on two of four wheels. We enjoyed the show so much, we decided to return each evening. The Royal York Hotel in downtown Toronto provided coaches to ferry guests to and from the exhibition. The hotel was a very grand multi-storey building and was honoured to have Queen Elizabeth and The Duke of Edinburgh stay there. Their portraits were displayed in the foyer. It was during the run up to the election campaign and the prime minister and many Canadian politicians were in residence in the Royal York. Their coach was sitting outside the hotel when Norman hopped on before it departed for the show. I heard the driver ask Norman if he was a member of the president's party. In a distinct Ulster accent, Norman apologised profusely and made a hasty retreat to wait for the next coach, hopefully one that was going to the show.

CHAPTER 19

The Irish Society

Our four children attended the Irish Society's Primary School in Coleraine. The first two, David and Ian, in the old building at Beresford Place and then at the new school on a green field site at Rugby Avenue. The transition went smoothly, although for Ian, it was one he will remember. The pupils had all moved into the new building on February 9, 1979. Ian and Daniel were great buddies in primary one, even though Daniel was a giant in stature compared to Ian. They had received permission to go to the toilet together. After a considerable time-lapse, Daniel returned sobbing to the classroom, followed by a sheepish boy who had *peed* over Daniel. Mrs Grant had been rather hassled by the move and was not too tolerant at that point, so she decided to send Ian to Mr Leitch, the headmaster. When he arrived home that afternoon Ian told me straightaway that he'd been sent to Mr Leitch's office. When I asked why, he assured me it was for doing good work, although I had my doubts. Later that month, Mrs Grant was sitting behind us at the panto in Coleraine Town Hall, when she leant forward. *"Did Ian tell you I sent him to the headmaster?"* she whispered in my ear. I told her he did tell me, but I was dubious as to the reason and the truth was then revealed. She told me she was at the end of her tether and just at that moment she had snapped but asked me not to remind Ian of the incident.

A little later in the summer, our family was in the outdoor swimming pool at Castlerock. Norman was at the deep end with David, while

Ian was at the shallow end, and I was perched against a wall, also at the shallow end, reading a book. I glanced up to see Ian exit the pool, pull down his swimming shorts and relieve himself into the swimming pool. He then nonchalantly pulled up his shorts and jumped in again. All the onlookers had a laugh and I joined in too.

The pupils left the final assembly in the historic red brick buildings in Beresford Place, which had been in use since 1869. Norman and his two brothers had attended this school many years before. The official opening of the new school by the governor of the Irish Society, Colonel & Alderman, the Right Honourable the Lord Mais of Walbrook GBE., ERD., TD., DL., D Sc., C.Eng. took place on Tuesday, June the 26, 1979. The architects of the school were PM Pollock B.Arch. P Laverty B. Arch. of W&M Given, a Coleraine firm, and the builders were Messrs T Linton and Co.

Both the plaque in the Irish Society's buildings in Beresford Place and the society's official history give 1705 as the date for the founding of the first school, but there is evidence to suggest that the Irish Society maintained a school in Coleraine from the seventeenth century; right from the first plantation. A free school was certainly in existence by 1679, when the society agreed that *'William Moute should keep school in the middle room of the courthouse free, keeping it in repair and giving security not to damage the courthouse.'* [22]

From 1739 to 1821, the school was probably situated on the south-west side of Kingsgate Street, though some records mention that the building was in ruins in 1814. In 1821, a new school was built on the commons in what is now Beresford Place and in the years 1867–69, the red brick building now facing Beresford Road was built. The inscription above the main entrance reads: *'Train up a child in the way he should go.'* In the years 1933–1935 the Irish Society greatly extended and modernised the buildings at Beresford Place, and they

---

[22] Taken from the opening of the new Irish Society's School brochure, June 26, 1979.

were officially reopened by Viscount Craigavon, DD., Prime Minister of Northern Ireland on July 17th, 1935. As the official history says, *The school was maintained and liberally supported by the society until it was taken over by the local education authority under the Northern Ireland Education Act of 1947. The society, however, continued its interest in visitations to the annual prize day. In February 1979, the pupils moved to the fine new building erected by the north-eastern education and library board, which in response to local sentiment continues to be known as the Irish Society's Primary School.*

The following is written of The Irish Society: *'The Irish Society has always maintained close links with Londonderry and Coleraine and today defines its role as custodian of the special relationship that still exists between the City of London and North Ulster. That relationship, in character and purpose, has undergone many changes through the centuries and has had to survive the strains and tensions of a troubled history [...] The Irish Society has always taken its own perpetuity, and the responsibilities and duties that go with that, very seriously. It cannot - and would not - will itself out of existence and walk away from a task that it believes so important and relevant.'* [23]

---

[23] https://honourableirishsociety.org.uk/about-us/our-history/

CHAPTER 20

Missing Children

It was a lovely sunny April morning and the potato planting had just commenced in the *'dam field.'* Norman was driving the tractor and planter and George, a farmhand, was rotovating the new ground alongside the planting. Suddenly, George lifted the machine out, then drove and bumped over the furrowed ground at speed. Norman saw what had happened and raced to the bottom of the field as the calamity unfolded. The International Hydro tractor had an unusual starting mechanism. There was no ignition key, and it was started with the gear lever. Ross, aged four, had got in the cab and somehow managed to start the tractor. A full trailer load, attached to the tractor, laden with boxed, well-sprouted seed potatoes was overturned and scattered across the field and the tractor was driven sideways into the hedge with the small driver lodged in the well of the tractor smiling from ear to ear. Mercifully, the tractor door was wedged closed, against the ditch. With an ashen face, Norman came down to the house to fetch help with the handling. After a good scolding all was put in place again, the work resumed and the potatoes yielded a good crop, despite some sprouts being detached at planting.

If I was busy in the kitchen and all was quiet in the living room, I could be sure that Ross was up to some mischief. True to form, when I investigated, there he was atop a chair with an egg whisk in the goldfish bowl, rotating it between two lovely orange specimens. Needless to say, they were beyond resuscitation.

On another day Ross tried to catch the caged canary in the living room. He had achieved his goal, but only to have nothing but the tail feathers left in his fist while the frightened bird cowered in its cage like a Manx cat. One time, when Auntie Jean was busy knitting (she was a wonderful Aran knitter), Ross decided to pull out a full row of stitches. Then there was the time when Nana and Auntie Jean were heading off to town as usual on a Thursday afternoon, when Ross invariably stood directly in front of her wee Austin A30 to delay them.

Ross was always a nuisance to his elder brothers in those days, although they are the best of friends now. David was often exasperated by him and suggested, *"Mum, I think you need to take him to see a psychiatrist."* Ross replied: *"Mum, I'll stay in the waiting room and send you in."*

One day as he was writing an essay for primary school, he asked me when Nana was born. After giving him the year, I asked why he was inquiring. *"Oh, I'm just writing about antiques and stuff,"* he replied. He used to like to stroke her cheek. *"Nana, I love your wrinkles,"* he'd say. His teacher in the Irish Society School asked how his dad got on with a bull he had entered at Balmoral Show, Belfast. *"Dad didn't get anything, but the bull got first prize,"* he replied. However, despite Ross's escapades in his youth, he later became a responsible civil servant and married Janet, who was also a civil servant. They jointly run a broiler chicken business and are the proud parents to teenagers Hannah and Ruby. Ross is meticulous in maintaining his home and gardens. He's a dab hand at pizza making and barbecuing too.

Ian became 'lost' on many occasions. One hot summer's day I had a visitor and once again Ian had disappeared. Only after a frantic search did I find him sitting crouched below a hedge, eating a pound of butter as the melted delicacy ran down his chin. One day, after another search, I found him some distance away with supplies for his dad who was ploughing. The basket contained a teapot, soda bread and biscuits.

When Ruth was in primary one, she was late returning home from school one day. A neighbour on the school run had dropped her off at the end of the lane, but instead of coming home she decided she would go to Pollock's shop to get a *Chronicle* for us and crisps for herself — without any money. She had to cross two roads to get to the shop. On her return home she placed her school bag on the kitchen table and produced her shopping. I immediately took her back to Ronnie and returned the items, asking him why he had given them to her, without being paid. He didn't get the point, and said he knew he would get paid okay.

One summer afternoon, Nana, the boys, Ruth and I went to Barry's in Portrush. After some rides Ruth could not be found. Initially, I didn't panic, but after a lengthy search by ourselves and the staff we still could not find her. I was about to call 999 when I decided I'd look in the car park in Eglinton Street across from the busy Portrush Road and completely out of bounds for a five-year-old. There she was, standing unconcerned beside our red car — and they say country children aren't street wise!

CHAPTER 21

Boys will be Boys

The events of 1982 were dominated by the Falkland Conflict between the UK and Argentina. Argentina invaded the Falklands on April 2nd, which lead to a British Task Force setting sail to reclaim the Islands. Britain declared a 200-mile 'exclusion zone' around the Falklands. On June 14th, the Falklands War ended as British Forces reached the outskirts of Stanley after *'yomping'*[24] across the East Falklands from San Carlos Bay (Bomb Alley). They arrived to find the Argentinian Forces waving white flags of surrender, which ended the 74-day Falkland Islands' Conflict.

Other events of 1982 include:

The Football World Cup in Spain was the biggest sports event of the year and Prince William was also born in that year.

In January, the lowest ever UK temperature was −27.2 degrees in Braemar, Aberdeen.

A pint of milk was 20 pence, butter was 44 pence per pound, ½ dozen brown eggs were 38 pence, Irish cheddar cheese 98 pence per pound.

Miners voted against strike action and accepted the National Coal Board offer of a 9.3% pay rise.

---

[24] Royal Marines slang describing a long-distance loaded march, carrying full kit.

The Queen celebrated her Pearl Jubilee.

The DeLorean car factory in Belfast and Antrim, famous for producing the car in the movie, Back to the Future, in Belfast, was put into receivership.

The twenty pence coin was introduced.

In the late seventies, along with other Northern Ireland farmers, we imported Charolais cattle, a continental breed which originated in west-central to south-eastern France, in the old French provinces of Charolles and neighbouring Nievre. To showcase the cattle, we entered the cattle at Balmoral Show in May each year, with a good deal of success. Because of the distance from Coleraine, Norman usually stayed for the duration of the show. It was during the show week in 1981, that I invited a few young neighbours to play with the boys on our farm. They speedily devoured their tea, eager to go outside again.

It wasn't long until Timothy came rushing into the kitchen to tell me that David had fallen off a wall. David was never the most adventurous of the boys, but this time he had acted as if he was Tarzan and had swung on a rope from the fourteen-foot silage wall, falling onto the concrete floor of the silage pit. As I rushed to the scene, I discovered David lying like a rag doll, motionless in a pool of red liquid. When I picked him up in my arms, I soon realised he'd had tomato sauce on his chips for tea, hence the red liquid. Tim's mum was summoned, and I rushed our ten-year-old into Coleraine A&E. The X-ray revealed that he had sustained a fractured skull, and he was admitted to the Children's Ward where he remained for a week. When I returned to visit him that evening, he was sitting up eating ice cream.

Despite his injury, he managed to pass his eleven-plus exam that year and head to Queens University Belfast and on to Aberdeen University. He had wonderful experiences during his student days. While in the Botany department at Queens in the summer, he visited a farmer in Fermanagh who had never applied fertilizer because the subsidy was suspended after World War II. During his inspection of a square metre of a meadow, David observed twenty species of wildflowers. The flora and fauna had been happily growing undisturbed for generations. As David talked with this eccentric character, he could almost see his reflection on his glazed bib overalls, which probably hadn't seen a wash tub in years. As they entered his humble abode, the improvised larder had a large bag hanging from the rafters and the laden table was groaning under the weight of utensils. David found it a delight to converse with this individual as he delivered his enigmatic descriptions and opinions on farming, but he was also equal fascinated by the remote area of Fermanagh.

The United Arab Emirates were *something else*, as David discovered while studying tropical diseases and dissected camels there. He learnt about a strange culture and had plenty of new experiences living with a family in Western Asia. It was an experience that is etched in his memory forever.

David visited Jamaica twice with a team from the Presbyterian Church in Ireland, when he worked with James and Pat Cameron at Mount Olivet Boys Home in Mandeville, while a student at Queens. Mount Olivet's vision statement was, '*To promote a loving, nurturing environment that will enable our children to be physically, spiritually, emotionally prepared to maximise their potential to make a worthwhile contribution to society.*' David maintained that under the guidance of the Camerons that statement was completely fulfilled.

On completing his master's degree in Aberdeen, he met Anna, his future wife and he now works as an animal nutritionist across Scotland and the Islands. They have two grown-up daughters Grace and Emma.

CHAPTER 22

I Can Face Tomorrow

Wednesday, March the 26th, 1980, our son David's birthday, was the dawning of a new era for Ballyrashane Church. Reverend Graham Connor (later to become Doctor Connor) received a unanimous call and was installed into our congregation. He succeeded Dr T H Mullin, who retired in September 1978. The deputation from Ballyrashane included Mr James Richmond, clerk of session, Mr Norman McClelland, treasurer, Mr Harry Adams, presbytery elder and Mr Ivan Carson. Reverend James Kane, convener of the vacancy formally welcomed the newly installed minister. Mr Connor thanked all who had attended the service and said it was particularly good to see members of his former congregations of Oldpark and Ballysillan in attendance. He added that he was looking forward to his work in Ballyrashane and thanked all those who worked so hard to make he and his wife — both *townies* — at home in the country. Mrs Mary Richmond presented Mrs Pat Connor with a bouquet of flowers. Mrs Connor then sincerely thanked the congregation for their welcome and especially the invaluable work that was done in the manse. Rev J V Craig from Ballysillan, reflected on Mr Connor's young days in the congregation there and congratulated Ballyrashane on their choice of minister. Reverend T Donnelly from Ballyclabber Reformed Presbyterian Church, and the Venerable Wilson, archdeacon of Dalriada, welcomed the new minister and his wife on behalf of the parishes of Ballyrashane and Kildollagh. Many other ministers brought greetings from across the presbyteries of the Presbyterian churches in Ireland. The offering at the service amounted to £550 for the student bursary fund.

Mr Connor was a breath of fresh air, after a lengthy vacancy. An addition to their family soon arrived with the birth of Sarah. It was lovely to have a new baby in the manse, and later Sarah attended Ballyrashane Primary School.

Although Pat was a town girl, she had a great liking for all things rural, and adapted wonderfully to her country setting. However, with the manse set among mature trees, it proved a bit eerie on dark winter evenings, especially with her being used to street lighting. As winter turned into spring, Pat acquired some laying hens. The hens laid well and one day, to Pat's delight, a broody hen strutted past with a line of yellow chicks behind her, having made her nest under a hedge in the manse garden. The next step was livestock and Cissy the goat was a further addition to the manse family. Cissy was very tame and when she got used to a tether and lead, Pat led her along Creamery Road to pick up Sarah from school - to the amusement of both the parents and children. I mentioned earlier how Pat helped us on the potato planter. As well as being an English graduate, she later took up nursing and social work. She was also a talented artist and gave me a lovely pencil drawing of a rose which she said was the meaning of my name *Diana*.

Graham became immersed in the pastoral care and scriptural teaching in Ballyrashane and proved to be a faithful pastor in every way, but it wasn't until about two years into his ministry that his sermons became much more pertinent to me. It was July 1982, and we had planned a family holiday to Malta, an archipelago in the Mediterranean Sea between Italy and Libya. I was looking forward to seeing Malta, knowing that it had over several thousand years of history, and contained some of the oldest, free-standing temples in the world. I was intrigued by its rich history, having hosted Phoenicians, Romans, the Knights of St John, Napoleon and the British Empire. However, two days before our departure, and unknown to anyone, I started to experience a terrible unease throughout my whole being. I was never keen on flying, but this was different. If the plane crashed, I wasn't afraid of being blown into smithereens. No, I was scared because I hadn't made my peace with God and I knew if I didn't, I would be lost forever. Despite this growing fear, we had a memorable holiday. Two or three days before my return home the same fear enveloped me, but still I was unable to share it with anyone.

The summer was over, and Norman had gone to a bull sale in Scotland when Mr Connor called to visit. With the family around us, our conversation was very general. I was keen to have my fears allayed by having a deep discussion with my minister, but *something* held me back. That following Christmas was a difficult one as I went through the motions of making it special for an enthusiastic family of four young children, yet I had no peace in my heart as I was very anxious about my spiritual state of existence.

Christmas was over and the decorations were placed in the roof space. Nana Ruby used to say there would be changes in another year. How true that turned out to be. It was a busy household, but we always managed to get to the mid-week Bible study and prayer meeting on Wednesday. Norman and I took it in turns to attend, and this was his night, but he was on a lengthy phone call, so he gestured for me to go to the meeting instead. Time was running out, so I hurriedly donned my coat and headed to the meeting that was to change my life forever.

The study concluded and the corporate prayer time began. There was much prayer for the needs of Ballyrashane congregation. Unbeknown to anyone present I had a lump in my throat and was almost overcome as I sensed that I needed more prayer than anyone else present at that meeting. As I made a hasty retreat with tears in my eyes, I decided to call at the manse. Sarah was tiny and Pat couldn't get to the mid-week. I had planned to go in by the upper gate, but reneged and eventually went in by the lower gate - with trembling and trepidation. We discussed many aspects of church life, and I shared my months of unrest and my fear of death.

I remember her asking me how long I'd been a Christian and I told her to her astonishment that I wasn't a Christian. *"Diana, I thought you were a Christian,"* she said. You see, like many, I put on a facade, doing all the churchy things: I was president of the Presbyterian Women's Association, attended mid-week meetings and I *'talked the talk.'* *"Diana, the Lord is working in your life, I know it by what you're saying,"* Pat said to me. In Psalm 34:8 it says, *'Taste and see that the Lord is good,'* (NIV). In the providence of God, Mr Connor was late home that night, which gave me time to have an in-depth discussion with Pat that ended with her leading me to the Lord and me making a commitment that was to change my life forever.

As the hymn by Keith Getty and Stuart Townend says, *'No guilt in life, no fear in death. This is the power of Christ in me. From life's first cry to final breath, Jesus commands my destiny. No power of hell, no scheme of man can ever pluck me from His hand, 'til he returns or calls me home, here in the power of Christ, I'll stand.'* [25]

Another verse of a hymn comes to mind, *'Because He lives, I can face tomorrow, because He lives, all fear is gone, because I know He holds the future and life is worth the living just because He lives.'* [26]

---

[25] In Christ Alone
[26] Because He Lives by Bill and Gloria Gaither

CHAPTER 23

A New Life to Start

Firstly, I need to tell you that I am not a spiritual expert or a great scholar in theology. But what I do have is a Christian conversion experience and I want to tell you about it. I know the word '*conversion*' might make some people uncomfortable, but it just means '*change*.' For example, some people these days, change their home central heating system to gas. Spiritual conversion is about a change from a self-centred life system to one that is Jesus-centred. Someone once said that becoming a Christian isn't a new start in life, but a new life to start — isn't that clever?

However, there are many who doubt whether Christian conversions are real. Let me tell you that if my conversion was in my imagination, then so is the chair that I'm sitting on. What happened to me in 1983 was not a figment of my imagination or a fantasy, but it was an experience that changed me from the inside out, altered me as a person, changing my attitudes, priorities and choices. I came to realise that living by my own efforts only resulted in failure. People say, *'I've tried Christianity, and it didn't work.'* Of course, it didn't work. Living the Christian life isn't something we try to do on our own. In fact, it's not about doing something, but about a Person we meet. In John 5 verse 12 we read, *"He who has the Son has life, he who has not the Son of God has not life"* (NIV). That is crystal clear. You either have Jesus in your life or you don't.

In January 1982, I was happily married with a family of four, ranging in age from four to eleven, when I first sensed a sort of incompleteness. It was as if I felt that there was something more to life which I didn't yet have, even though I had so much going for me. In the Old Testament Book of Isaiah, we read, *"But the wicked are like the tossing sea, which cannot rest, whose waves cast up mire and dirt, he says"* Isaiah 57.20-21 (KJV). That very much reflects what I was going through.

That night in Ballyrashane manse, life took on a completely new meaning for me; the void in my life was being filled. After a short period, while I was still a fledging Christian, I realised that I needed to be stimulated and built up in my faith. Our minister, Reverend Graham Connor was at the ready, and he introduced me to a discipleship course published by The Navigators to equip new believers, of which I was one. The theme verse was from Colossians 2:6-7, *'So then, just as you received Christ Jesus as Lord, continue to live in Him, rooted and built up in Him, strengthened in the faith you were taught and overflowing with thankfulness'* (NIV). It took place over a two-year period and included quite a bit of discipline to complete. It was useful to each member of the group, which consisted of ten women. You had to highlight and share a particular portion of scripture and recite a memorised verse each week. With a young family it was difficult, but I valued my quiet time of communion with God each morning.

There were many more opportunities to help me mature in my faith. Just like my secular business, where I always had to keep on learning, I also had to study and be involved in Bible studies to develop and grow in my faith. One such study was held in the Sandel Centre, Coleraine. It was a satellite programme from Belfast Bible College, with various class tutors throughout the year. A friend and I also travelled to Belfast to undertake a *Level 1 and 2 Christian Counselling Foundation Course*, which later proved very beneficial.

Of course, I received wonderful teaching from the pulpit Sunday by Sunday, as well as mid-week Bible study and prayer. I had a great appetite for Bible study and wouldn't miss the mid-week meeting or church on Sunday. I should add, it was never a ritual, and I wasn't '*pious,*' but I had an appetite to learn about God and His Son Jesus, an appetite that has never been quenched since and always increases. It deepens my spiritual life, thus making me more able to help others in the work and witness of our church. I am very aware of the great needs that exist in our community today and pray daily for wisdom in my thinking, speaking and interacting with others. I hope I will always be honourable and pleasing to my Heavenly Father.

Since making that important decision to follow Jesus all the days of my life, I thank those faithful mentors who took me under their wing and supported me in prayer. I will be forever grateful to them.

I must be honest and say that since my conversion, life hasn't always been a '*bed of roses,*' as you will have read. There were risks attached to my new-found faith and I faced many difficulties. The risk of being jeered at, the risk of being left out of a party — and these things have happened. But *real faith* involves real risks. Since coming to faith, I have learnt to believe that God works in mysterious ways and His ways are not our ways. As a Christian, I must be honest, there were times I wondered what God was doing to me. But, in retrospect, I can see He is working out His wise purposes for my good. There are purposes and values in life and at the centre there is a God who cares, and I'm encouraged as I look back and see His hand in everything. God uses life's reverses to move us forward, and I have proved that many times.

I have always found Jesus to be a faithful friend who never leaves me to cope on my own. Someone once said, '*The person who ceases to be better, ceases to be good.*' I know that if I am not growing closer to Jesus in my daily life, I will gradually slip away from Him. God wants our faith in Him to grow. To be a healthy and stable Christian, I must feed on His Word daily and let Him be in control of every area of my life. I quote a lovely promise from Psalm 138:8, '*The Lord will fulfil His purpose for me; Your love, O Lord endures forever do not abandon the works of your hands'* (NIV).

Jesus's words in the last book of the Bible in Revelation 3.20 are for you. *"'Behold I stand at the door and knock"*, says Jesus. *"If anyone hears My voice and opens the door, I will come in to him"'* (ESV). This is a promise, and it is unambiguous. All I can do is commend my Friend Jesus to you. If you are conscious of Him knocking you should respond. There will be a new dimension of life ahead for you. I look forward in faith to the day when many of my friends, and family from age nine to ninety, will come to put their trust in this same Jesus, whom I have trusted and who has never failed me over these last forty years.

CHAPTER 24

Constable Tracy Doak

Hundreds stood in the heavy rain to pay their respects to Constable Tracy Doak, a twenty-one-year-old female officer who was killed, along with three of her colleagues, in a massive bomb attack at Killeen outside Newry, on May the 20th, 1985. We knew the Doak family well as they lived about a mile from us at Ballindreen. Tracy's mother Jean was well known in Soroptimist circles and was a member of New Row Badminton Club, of which Norman was also a member. They travelled up and down the country to matches. Tracy came from a well-respected police family, her father, Beattie, and her brother were both serving officers in the Royal Ulster Constabulary (RUC).

Before the church service Mr Hunter conducted a short service in the family home at Ballindreen and the cortege. The RUC Silver Band made its way along the tree-lined avenue to the roadway, where Tracy's colleagues had assembled to form a guard of honour. The Union Jack draped-coffin on which was placed Constable Doak's hat, was carried for some distance along the narrow country roads, with members of the RUC acting as pall bearers, as the cortege made its way to Ballywatt Presbyterian Church. Leading the mourners were WPC Doak's father, Beattie, her brother Allister and her fiancée, all serving members of the RUC. Her distraught mother, Mrs Jean Doak, was comforted by her grieving daughters, Amanda and Alison. Tracy's great grandmother and grandparents were also present.

In paying tribute, Reverend Ivan Hunter, minister of Ballywatt Presbyterian Church, said of Tracy, *"She was a genuinely warm person, who, because of her warmth and the outgoing nature of her personality, made friends wherever she went."* He continued, *"Tracy knew the dangers she faced, accepted the risks and went about her duty to do her best in the service of the community. I know personally she often felt deeply a sense of rejection and opposition, which some in our land show to police officers. But she wished nothing more than to serve the public and uphold the law of the land without fear ... she bore no grudge towards anyone, but simply wished to get on with the task of carrying out her duties as a police officer. Isn't that what we want to see in our policemen and policewomen – dedication to duty? Isn't that one of the essential qualities in every good police officer? Yet in attempting to do that, Tracy and many others have been killed by an unseen enemy, by 'faceless' men who do their deeds in secret and in hiding. My friends, we must uphold the bravery of these brave men and women who serve in our police force, stepping out into the front rank of danger so that others may have security ... we must never let them down."*

The Very Reverend Dr Ronald Craig, a former moderator of the Presbyterian Church, extended the sympathy of the Presbyterian Church Families worldwide and in doing so, Dr Craig added what he termed as, *"My own sense of revulsion and sorrow at the callous and shocking murders."*

The whole Presbyterian Church, throughout the province was thinking of Ballywatt, particularly the bereaved family. *"Sunday after Sunday, we offer prayers for people in circumstances such as we have today, but only when it comes right to our doorstep, do we know the full effect of it. Let us be conscious that throughout our land, not only are the members of our church, but of others, seeking to uphold you in prayer."*

Dr Craig also paid tribute to the dedication which WPC Doak showed to her service in her community within the ranks of the RUC and said that following in the footsteps of her father and brother, she felt she had a proud heritage. *"Our sympathy goes out to the members of the whole force, especially to Tracy's colleagues in the Newry area who have suffered so terribly in recent years. I personally have just returned from Malawi, a land made up of tribes, which for centuries were massacring each other, and yet today they are living in harmony and peace, so that people speak of Friendly Malawi. Surely the industrious, warm-hearted people in this land, far outnumber the heinous murderers who are hell bent on the destruction of our beloved country and we can work together to bring an end to this era of tragedy and heartbreak. There is one thing above all others that has transformed Malawi, that has been the missionary influence of the last hundred years. The result should be plain for us, we all need to get back to a serious acknowledgement of God's rule in every department of life ... social, political and religious."*

How that rings true today in this generation, nearly thirty years later.

After the final hymn, How Great Thou Art, Constable Doak's coffin was borne to the adjoining graveyard by members of her family, and after a short committal service, she was laid to rest beside the church where she was to be married in September. Among the many floral tributes placed on the grave were several from her colleagues in the RUC and one from her parents which had the name Tracy in pink flowers against a white background. The following poem was dedicated to Coleraine Soroptimist President Mrs Jean Doak from a Soroptimist friend, who said, *"In this year of International Goodwill and Understanding I would give these thoughts to Tracy and all the victims of violence in Northern Ireland."*

*Tracy Ellen is gone, she is resting in peace
May the memory of her goodness never cease
To be remembered by all whom this soul I knew
Before she was buried beneath the dew
Only twenty-one when she lost her life
Yet her only wish in this land of strife
Was to live her life as a Christian should
That was why she was kind and good*

She did not deserve a bitter end
For Christ forgive, for no one can defend
The evil thoughts that brought to an end
This little flower, who on a spring day
Blossomed and died upon the highway

To her parents dear what can I say
About what happened on that dreadful day?
The God of Love will near them stay
And consolation bring each day
Listen awhile to what He might say
Oh, why take an innocent life away?
You who will not heed the truth
You who destroy and corrupt the youth
Know you not that it isn't My will
That My creatures should bomb and main and kill?
This is no part of My Holy plan
Such is devised by the will of man
Like those who preferred Barabbas to me
The same who nailed Me to a tree
Where I died for love of all

Sweet Spirit of Christ, we beg for Grace
To overcome this dreadful disgrace
Which has been our lot to witness and bear
Save us Lord from dire despair
Oh, risen Christ we need you so
Look with pity here below
Inflame our hearts with your changeless love
Bear with us, Oh Gentle Dove
That strife may end and murders cease
As we accept the Prince of Peace
The man of love on a spring day
Blossomed and died on a hill far away
… thy will be done, thy Kingdom come.

CHAPTER 25

The Light Bulb Moment

I n 1998 a visit to the Royal Agricultural Show at Stoneleigh Warwickshire was a first for our family. The boys enjoyed the opportunity to participate in the *Junior Stock -Judging Competition* at such a prestigious venue! Norman and the boys went around the cattle, sheep enclosures and trade stands, while Ruth and I walked around the vast exhibition areas.

I must have seemed interested as the chairman of the N Ireland CC approached me. The Camping and Caravan Club was founded in 1901 in the United Kingdom and became a new form of camping and caravanning. At that time there were only a few certified CC sites in Northern Ireland and none on the North Coast. He was very keen that we should have further discussions about the possibility of us providing a site on our farm. I honestly put it to the back of my mind and didn't think of mentioning it to Norman, until one autumn afternoon on my return, when I was met by a dismayed and startled (to say it mildly!) husband! *"Who was the 'oul' white haired man who came asking about having caravans on the farm?"* he asked me. I had learned my first mistake, to always discuss everything with my husband, no matter how trivial, anything relating to the farm!

He was fit to be tied, when I told him that all that was required was the wee 2-acre field across the drive from our house, a standpipe for water, and a waste disposal drain for a chemical disposal, which could be connected to our domestic sewer. I had eyed out the field for some time, but there were a few legislations to also be considered. We were only allowed 5 vans at any given time, and they were only permitted to stay for 28 days, otherwise planning permission had to be sought. Norman eventually conceded to my idea and in a short time my small enterprise was up and running and we welcomed 60 vans from the Caravan Club for a weekend in Spring 1991. It seemed like no problem - a nice level field, 5 vans, no planning necessary, and a 28 day stay! Norman did simmer a tad when the first caravan appeared on the site! As I said before, we had only one caravan holiday and that was primitive. Norman had said it would be our last and he kept to his word!

The weather was favourable that summer at Tullans, and we had full occupancy (5 vans) for our first season! On our way to a BBQ at Greenmount Agricultural College, Antrim, I embarked on my first market research exercise! I counted the number of touring caravans we met coming up to the North Coast, over a distance of around 40 miles. I then made enquiries about the local existing Caravan Touring sites and found that the demand for spaces outstripped supply. I realised that a bigger site with more facilities would be more attractive for families and, given that we are only 6 miles from the coast, on a working farm, I felt there was a niche in the market for a rural family run site, convenient to Portrush, Portstewart, Castlerock and the Causeway Coast. I wasn't planning to compete with the large commercial sites, as they are not to everyone's taste.

I was never a feminist, but at that time the odds were often stacked against women. In addition to all the normal pressures of running a business, they often had to face the added responsibilities of managing a family and, dare I say it, dealing with prejudice in what some would consider to be very much a man's world. There were naysayers around the countryside who weren't overly keen on what I was doing. One neighbour quipped, *"I see McClellands have wigwams now!"* A National Opinion Poll in the nineties in a survey of businesses start-ups found that men tended to over-estimate their turnover, while women were much more conservative, often under-estimating their eventual turnover. Consequently, a woman's business often became profitable sooner!

I was beginning to feel my dream was becoming a reality. However, my husband interpretation was very different! "*What! Give up 2 acres for caravans? You must be mad! Anyway, who'd come here? There's no beach nor sea!*" *Little* did he think that some years later, customers would be recording a cow at every stage of labour, photographing sheep lambing, feeding pet lambs, looking on when sheep shearing was carried out and painting an Irish hare in the grass! I plodded on with my plans regardless.

I had been operating a successful Bed and Breakfast for some years and felt the caravan site could work well alongside the B&B. At this point I hadn't many business skills, I was sure there was more to a business than just having a good idea, so I enrolled on the *Women in Business Programme* at Coleraine Enterprise Agency. This was followed by a course at the University of Ulster, Coleraine entitled *Micro Computers and Applications*.

In a frosty and snowy January, I travelled to Ballybofey in Co. Donegal, where I had been selected to participate on a *Wider Horizions Project for a Cross Border Farm Diversification Programme*. At the conclusion of the course, I had the opportunity of field trips to visit similar projects in the Republic of Ireland and in Scotland. This was a very worthwhile exercise, as I gleaned many tips and ideas from different caravan parks. All the courses were practical and fun, not only lectures, but useful exercises, with guest speakers and discussion groups included. I remember well John Armstrong of Armstrong Medicals speaking to our class at Coleraine Enterprise Agency. He shared with us how he had given up his secure job as a medical Rep to launch his own career into the manufacture of medical respiratory products etc. He told us that his wife was really worried about his decision because he had to give up his company car! Armstrong Medicals has turned into a world-wide business with a turnover of £14m. John founded the firm in 1984 and sold it to Eakin Healthcare in 2020.

I don't think I could have approached my bank manager with the same assertiveness, had I not undertaken these invaluable courses. At this stage I was using terms like market research, business plans, spread sheets and cash flow. Prior to this, I had assumed that cash flow was the money the teller spread out in front of you at the bank desk!

To enhance my facilities, I had to include a shower block, with toilet, laundry facilities and a recreational area. Across the farm drive from the C L site, there was a 6-acre site adjoining a long disused deep litter house. Again, I met an obstacle, *"I definitely can't let you have the lambing shed,"* Norman said. This however was a suitable level site and perfect for caravans! But it was a much bigger project, requiring planning approval for the relocation and the conversion of the deep litter house (lambing shed) to an amenity block. The wheels were set in motion with hubby still very nervous at giving over 6 acres for a caravan site!

Because our farm was on a green belt, I had many debates and countless meetings with the Planning Department, who continually threw obstacles in my way. Some argued that a caravan park would not contribute to the economy of the area. How wrong they proved to be! Every single caravanner brings revenue into the area in many ways, spending their money in shops, at leisure centres, golf courses and at restaurants. Eventually the committee conceded, and we were granted permission after a 4-year uphill battle with officialdom! When the planning problem was overcome, the wheels were set in motion.

The next step on my entrepreneurial journey was to my local bank manager. I felt quite confident as I arrived with my business plan under my arm. As I presented my proposed project to the Manager and his Deputy, I was confidently hopeful. My accountant advised me to keep it a separate entity to the farm business. Horror of horrors, my projected figures were based on my income from the B&B business and a small policy which was due to mature in a few months. However, after a lengthy discussion, I received a very positive response, and they gave me permission to proceed. On the strength of their approval, I bought roof trusses for the amenity block.

The following Monday, I received a phone call, followed by a letter, to inform me that my proposal was turned down at Head Office in Belfast. They said it was too big a risk! What was I to do? Norman came on the scene to defuse the situation and said *"We'll get it sorted, we can sell some bullocks and that'll fix it."* There was a *'softie'* below his skin! The following week was the Balmoral Show and Norman bumped into the business manager of our bank and shared my dilemma with him. He told him he couldn't understand that the local branch manager could sign off an arrangement, only to later be reversed by Headquarters! I had prayed to God that if it wasn't His will that the project should proceed, I would accept it. I believe in Divine Intervention, for on the following Monday, 3 weeks after the initial phone call and letter from that same bank manager in Coleraine, the same person quoted a verse from Romans 10:15 *'How beautiful are the feet of those who bring good news.'* I could hardly take in what I was hearing from a secular institution! He told me there was a turnaround, my plan was accepted, and I could proceed with my project! I still have the original fateful letter in my file!

You see, if you have the enthusiasm and faith, you'll convince people eventually - whether that's your family, your bank manager or yourself! It was Peter Drucket who said, *'In this world, you don't get what you deserve, you get what you negotiate!'* Negotiate I did and I was ready for action! The thrill and success and the pride of developing and nursing a trading entity through good times and bad times is a unique feeling, which the succeeding generation is entitled to have the opportunity to share!

One of our difficult times was when the builder, who was cutting out the spaces in the outer wall to accommodate doors and windows for the amenity block, discovered the inner wall was built for insulation purposes at a later date and had no foundation, so it started to shake. He asked me to call Building Control, who on examination said the wall would have to be torn down and a foundation dug to accommodate a new 70 metre wall! Norman came on the scene as the problem was surveyed and had to be built for an additional cost of £1,000. After a cup of tea to recover from the shock he said, *"This thing is going to put us out of the farm!"* Thankfully that was the only hiccup that occurred!

June 1991 was supposed to see the completion date, but it was August and almost the end of the summer when we opened the gates to a handful of caravanners to visit our pristine toilets, showers, laundry room, TV lounge and indoor games hall. We also had an outdoor play area and 40 electric hook ups, to include 6 static sites, all with concrete bases. I was very fortunate to meet an environmental officer who was a member of the Caravan Council and owned a small caravan park in Co Down. He suggested I should consider having some static vans which would help our cash flow as the owners paid their fees in January, before the touring season began. I went back to planners with my proposal to hit a brick wall! However, I asked for eight static caravans and they granted me six. The timing was perfect as the Marina Caravan park in Coleraine was closing and I acquired my first six customers from there. Incidentally, some of them are still with us!

I distributed promotional flyers at Holiday Fairs and Exhibitions at various venues across the province and then sat at the living room window and counted------and yes, our first season had been a good one! At bank holidays and peak times, we had 100 per cent occupancy. In the autumn of 1998, I attended a *GROW (Growing Real Opportunities for Women)* programme in Derry/Londonderry. I did a market overview to include various areas of my business, competitor analysis, promotional literature, and market opportunities on the World Wide Web. I also joined seminars on a Family Business Executive Programme at the University of Ulster, where many problems and solutions were addressed, all proving most helpful in the running of a family business.

Because of my participation in some of these initiatives, I was invited to go on a European study tour to The Louvain Institute for Ireland in Europe, along with 24 other participants. It was organised by Coleraine Local Action Group for Enterprise (C.O.L.A.G.E.) of which I was a board member. We arrived on the 9th of May 2000 in Brussels Charleroi

Airport for a programme of four days. On the day prior to our departure, we had the privilege of visiting the European Parliament in Brussels where we learned of the work and role of the European Parliament and met two of our MEPs at a lunch in the Parliament Restaurant. We then departed for the Northern Ireland Centre in Europe and had free time in Brussels. On our return to Leuven, we enjoyed an Aperitif and Banquet, then retired to bed. After breakfast the next day, we departed for Brussels Charleroi Airport for our return journey home with many happy memories of a very worthwhile trip.

A few years later, after many enquiries, I applied for an extension to the static site. After endless debates and intense interviews with the Planning Authorities, permission was granted for an additional 28 vans. This probably all sounds easy, but there are many risks in setting up a business. It may not be easy, but it is very rewarding! The touring site is the shop window for the statics as they are linked into the sewer and beds are made up. From the outset, I wanted to establish high standards and from day one I insisted that we had to give a highly professional service to our customers if we were to have them come back. It obviously paid off, as 90 per cent of our business was repeats. Our customers told others and so our best and cheapest advertisement was by word of mouth!

Mother Teresa of Calcutta (Born in Macedonia) was once asked how she would describe the type of person she desired to work alongside her in the dark alleyways of Calcutta. She replied, *"[Those who] have a desire to work hard and have a heart for people!"*

I was warned to never rest on my laurels, to always be aware of your competitors and always strive to be a step ahead of them. In 1996 Tullans was the only rural park on the North Coast, now there are five on the North Coast, including one other on a working farm. However, I could not be happy to just keep my head above water and meet all my financial commitments. No, that wasn't how to run a business successfully. I realised more and more that I had to periodically take an overview of my whole business - looking at the bigger picture, such as cost control, marketing, cash flow - all important elements of my business. Uncontrolled cost can be lethal in any business. Do I put a cost on my travel and time? My time management was difficult as people were on holiday, and they had all the time in the world and wanted a chat - sometimes a lengthy one at that!

Marketing was very important as there could be occupancy gaps during the shoulder months and midweek, so I introduced *'stay 7 get 1 free'* or *'over 50s'* reduction in June and September. I set myself some short- and long-term objectives for my business. A computer was purchased to save time and money. I increased my fees by an annual increase in line with inflation, with no customer complaints! They expected high standards and were willing to pay up! Someone once said, *'Why buy a Mini if you can afford a Rolls Royce!'*

I couldn't rest on my laurels until I had arrived. But I did arrive, and Tullans Farm developed into a thriving business, geared to serve its customers effectively and profitably into the next Millennium. There is much to be gained by partnership and I already had embarked on a partnership with my counterparts in the Republic and mainland Great Britain. Partnership is a concept which neatly embraces its philosophy of cooperation, working together to our mutual benefit. My mission statement was: *'Tullans Farm - for Peace and Tranquillity, Where People Matter.'*

My advice is always to be positive, even when everyone is against you! If your bank manager or planning officer turn you down, don't be deterred, go back again and again. Never be pessimistic, as that's the rock you'll perish on! Seriously, if you have problems, I realised that there is always plenty of help available. Even your bank manager is happy to give you help and advice, and if you are honest, he will be fair with you. Don't be like that pessimistic man, whom, when asked how his business was going, replied, *"I'm having a middling year; worse than last year, but not as bad as what next year is going to be."*

I wonder what your goals or dreams are? Are they clear enough to write down? Strong enough to help you persevere and valuable enough to be worth the price you might pay? If they are, you will see your dreams become a reality and all your ambitions fulfilled. But even if your project fails, the very fact that you tried, in a way, makes you successful. As Eleanor Roosevelt said, *"The future belongs to those who believe in the beauty of their dreams."* [27]

I have heard that 50% of the people you know don't know where they're going. Another 40% will go in any direction they are led. The remaining10% know where they'd like to go, but half of them will never pay the price to get there!

I always strived to create balance and to concentrate on the things that were important. Money is important, but it doesn't mean anything if you can't take time to enjoy it! Prioritizing my time was very important to me, albeit difficult at times. I would stress the importance of taking time out to attend courses and programmes on self- development. These are very important to any business as you can learn much from the other participants, as well as the course itself. I availed of all the courses I could get my hands on!

At one of my courses, I became friendly with a farmer's wife from Torr Head, near Ballycastle. At the end of the course, she invited me along to see her husband's collection of vintage farm machinery. I was mesmerised at his extensive range of collectibles, including 6 red telephone boxes and sought to buy one. After haggling persistently for a while, we eventually agreed on a price! What about transport? He said I would need a flat trailer!

Our good neighbour Tom McClure came to the rescue and, with Norman for help, he set off with ropes and chain on the flat trailer

---

[27] Bella Grace… Eleanor Roosevelt Quotes To Live By.

hitched to the Land Rover, for the valuable specimen, which I assured them was a collector's item! The telephone box obviously had been extracted from the ground with a digger and had a huge deep concrete base attached. The box was securely loaded, and they set off along the winding road that is Torr Head. All was going well until Norman pressed the accelerator too robustly going downhill, The front of the Land Rover was airborne and the trailer took a few sways sideways. Thankfully Norman got it back on track again with very few words being spoken for the remainder of the journey back. Tom arrived back at Tullans like someone who'd had a nasty bout of seasickness.

The box had pride of place at the front of the amenity block and proved useful for many years, until a few young rascals dialled 999 with monotonous regularity, and the police arrived to find it was a hoax call! About that time, mobile phones began to be popular, so the red box became redundant and was assigned a place on its side in the back yard. It became a project for a later date, requiring sandblasting and painting to bring it back to its former glory!

I cannot continue without mentioning my dear mother-in-law Ruby, who was behind me at every turn. She did everything within her power to encourage and help me along the way. Of course, in time Norman became a wonderful helpmeet to me and I could not have provided a better Ranger as he liaised with customers whilst touring the park on his Quad, and later his Polaris! *"It wasn't a bad idea,"* he was heard to say!!!

CHAPTER 26

Our B&B

I t was in the late 80's when I embarked on an adventure which opened a whole new world to me and my family. The guests at our B&B came from all over the world - from Torquay to Tasmania, from Switzerland to Spain, from Nebraska to the Netherlands and from Japan to Jerusalem, and many places in-between. I remember well a lovely guest from Japan. She had come one night, solely to visit an Irish Dancing Festival in Portrush. As I left her to catch the train in Coleraine, I discovered she had a prosthetic arm. Yet there she was with a rucksack and a heavy case making her way around the country.

On another occasion a lady from Guernsey came rushing to my door after an early morning walk. *"Have I seen a fox?"* she asked me, with great excitement. Apparently, there are no foxes in Guernsey, and this was a new experience for her.

I had a weird experience with one guest. She was a German artist, and on my first encounter I found her rather eccentric, with a rugged appearance, and her hair tied in a loose bun. She informed me that she would be up early for a walk and asked for an early cooked breakfast. She had paid me on arrival and a time for breakfast was arranged. The time came and went and there was no sign of my guest. I waited for quite a while before knocking on her door with bated breath. When there was no response, I eased open the door and found the room empty. Like Goldilocks, the bed had been slept in, but no one was there; I was at a loss to know what to do. Did I phone the police to inform them of a missing person or did I ignore the mystery? I did the latter and never heard from my strange guest again.

A lovely couple from Holland came to stay while they were on their honeymoon. The husband was a cartoonist and when they left, he gave us a sketch of Norman wearing his flat cap and leaning on a stick.

Talking of pictures, during our visit to St Jacobs in Ontario, I purchased a needlepoint kit with a *'welcome'* picture in the Mennonite style. The Mennonites are a group of Anabaptists with Swiss origins. They formed during the Reformation in the sixteenth century. The Amish are more conservative Anabaptists, while the Mennonites are their more moderate, progressive cousins, accepting of modern technology, while maintaining a strong commitment to their faith.

I always had the illusion that I was keen on craft work. To be fair I was often enthusiastic to begin a project, but slow to get it completed. So, the needlepoint picture began with the same gusto, only to be consigned to a place in the roof space. A Scottish couple visited us annually and the conversation came around to needlecraft, at which the woman was very proficient. On bemoaning the fact that I had abandoned the unfinished picture, she offered to take it back with her and return the finished article on her next visit. In the first instance I couldn't find it, but after a frantic search the prodigal item was recovered. She returned with the completed article, and it now graces our hall wall to welcome all our visitors. The only problem is, when it is admired, I have to confess that I received help with its completion.

One elderly guest came often, and as I became more familiar with her, a great bond grew between us. One day during a discussion about why some people don't come to faith, she in her wisdom explained: *"You see, the snowdrops bloom in January and February, roses bloom in June and chrysanthemums bloom in October and God moves in people's lives at different times."* I have never forgotten those words of wisdom.

I vividly recall Mickey from Donegal who operated a minibus to transfer golfers, usually Americans, from Donegal to the famous golf courses around the north coast. He was a gifted conversationalist, full of wit and Irish charm. He and Norman *'clicked'* well, and both enjoyed the craic. I could see why he boasted of the generous tips he received from his wealthy passengers. He was probably a tad economical with the truth at times when he relayed yarns and stories, transporting his passengers to a level of folktales, myths and legends, the likes of which they had never heard before.

I remember another couple with two children who came from County Offaly. One evening we were deeply engrossed in conversation when Peter, who was talking about a serious accident in which he was injured, referred to various Scripture verses. Knowing he was from the Catholic faith, I suggested he could be a teacher or philosopher. *"I studied the priesthood for five years,"* he replied. The other guests were all astounded and curious as to why he was married. His honest and interesting reply came when he explained his reason. He was in a strict seminary from which they travelled by minibus to Dublin once a month. *"We were crossing a bridge and there was a row of girls sitting on a wall and I realised the priesthood wasn't for me,"* he said. The rest, as they say, is history. I have to say he didn't renounce his faith but was firm in his conviction against celibacy in the priesthood. These late-night conversations were most enjoyable, but chores needed to be completed for the next morning; and so sometimes I had to call *'lights out'* and lock up for the night.

Those were very valuable years on life's journey, and I learnt much about different cultures. Initially, the cooked breakfast didn't always run smoothly. Having to fry four eggs before getting a perfect *'sunny side up'* was not always easy. The usual Ulster fare included porridge, cereal, fruit compote, bacon, eggs, sausages, tomatoes, mushrooms, potato bread *(Fadge)* and soda bread. In those days there were very few guests who dismissed the *'Ulster Fry.'* Just a few opted for the healthy option of yogurt, or a continental breakfast. Most folk felt that a cooked breakfast set them up for the day.

When the caravan park was up and running, it worked in tandem with the guest house and provided accommodation for extra friends who wanted to stay in the area. We were affiliated to the Farm Bureau and received many bookings from that association, as well as the Northern Ireland Farm Guesthouse. There was a great liaison between fellow guest-house owners in the area, and when they had full occupancy, they contacted other premises to find vacancies for would-be guests.

The Farm Guest House members held an annual meeting, which was usually in Loughry Agricultural College, and it was always a useful meeting to compare notes and obtain an update on the current state of the hospitality industry. Our local guest house owners also met socially throughout the year and exchanged many interesting and amusing anecdotes — all very different from one another. As I look over my visitors' book of twenty years, which I treasure, I do so with nostalgia and wistful affection for a period in the past which will never be erased from my memory.

CHAPTER 27

"Allergic to Cats" he said.

Not in my wildest dreams did I ever imagine that the caravan park would open such a world of opportunities. I met some very interesting people from all over the world. Many came as strangers and went home as friends. It was a wonderful way of telling them our story, informing them of the local attractions, and promoting our beautiful north coast.

The working farm was an added bonus. I remember well when a customer came to my door to tell me there were two lambs lying dead in a field adjoining the caravan park. I went out to examine the scene to find that the wee lambs were basking at their length in the sunshine. On many occasions the camera with the zoom lens was brought into focus to capture every stage of labour as a cow was ready to deliver a new-born calf. Again, they were alarmed that we allowed nature to take its course and only intervened when necessary. I think many onlookers went through the pain along with the cow! For many years the visitors enjoyed the sheep shearing season and the children were delighted to feed the pet lambs. Unfortunately, because of insurance issues and the risks attached to allowing visitors to the farm, it is no longer possible to allow access on to the farm. However, they can still get a taste of rural living when the slurry is spread on fields adjacent to the park.

Oddly enough, cats caused some havoc in our caravan park. Once, a customer knocked on my door to inform me that our cat had eaten their cooked chicken. On making further enquiries, I discovered that they had placed the chicken in their awning, so it was fair game for a roaming farm feline lured to the tasty treat. Another day a gentleman came to tell me his wife was allergic to cats. I tried to explain that when he came to a farm, he surely must have realised it was not a disinfected farm and that there would most definitely be cats about the place. Indeed, there were two or three around the park, and they were much more favourable than having vermin scurrying around. I think we lost a customer.

We also had a stray cat come to visit. It looked very much like a Russian Blue. It was very thin and needed food. I fattened it up over the ensuing months, and later it produced a substantial litter of kittens. Because of the increase in the cat population at Tullans, Ross and his dad decided to deliver some to the local NSPCA shelter. Well, that was a noisy task to execute. The two volunteers donned gloves and put a cage in place, then tried with the greatest of effort to cage the cats. After screeches from both Ross and Norman, and squeals from the petrified cats themselves, the mission was duly completed. After that episode, the cat population was monitored on a six-monthly basis, and I was forbidden to take in any more refugees. There were many funny incidents over the years, too many to mention here.

There were great opportunities to give a listening ear to people who wanted to share their story, some happy and some heart-rending. I was conscious that I needed to build time into my business, although it wasn't always easy, with a busy household to manage. But from the outset I was very conscious that people were at the heart of my business, and I was determined never to forget that fact. It did pay off. As I work in my retirement in my garden and caravanners walk past, they often stop and have a chat, for old times' sake. Some of these caravanners come from thirty years back. The problem is names sometimes elude me now.

A lovely opportunity came my way in 1991. I was nominated for the *Bank of Ireland Farm Women's Award* (See below) and was overwhelmed when I was declared a finalist. That led to a trip to Dublin for the presentation ceremony of a beautiful, framed citation and a text overview of my caravan site project. It was also a privilege to engage with other businesswomen from various farming backgrounds across Ireland. It was a momentous occasion, and the presentation took place in the Bank of Ireland in College Green, a three-sided plaza in the centre of Dublin. On its northern side is the Bank of Ireland building, which until 1800 was Ireland's Parliament House. To its east stands Trinity College, and to the south stands a series of beautiful nineteenth-century buildings.

***

The Bank of Ireland is a building steeped in history. It was founded in 1783, and today has 9,074 employees. It first opened for business at Mary's Abbey in a private house owned by Charles Blakeney. In 1803 it moved to Parliament House in Dublin. Parliament House was built in 1729, of Palladian Architecture. The building was home to the two houses of parliament, and served as the seat of both chambers, the Lords and Commons, of the Parliament of the Kingdom of Ireland for most of the eighteenth century until that parliament was abolished by the Act of Union of 1800, when Ireland became part of the United Kingdom of Great Britain and Ireland. The building is fascinating and contains much symbolism. The ceremonial mace of the House of Commons remained in the family descendants of John Foster, the last Speaker of the House, until a sale at Christie's in London in 1915, when the Bank of Ireland bought the Mace for £3,000. The chair of the speaker of the House of Commons is now in the possession of the

Royal Dublin Society, while the bench from the commons is in the Royal Dublin Academy. The two original tapestries are fascinating and remain on the walls in the House of Lords, and the Bank of Ireland. They were designed by Dutch landscape painter Willem Van der Hagen, and woven by John Van Beaver. These tapestries are unique and priceless, and date from 1733. One represents the Battle of the Boyne and the other the Defence of Londonderry. Each tapestry has five portrait and narrative medallions around the central scene, which depict, narrate and name central characters and events in the battles. Both also have trophies of arms and figures of fame below and are enclosed by fringed curtains. The wonderful chandelier from the House of Commons hangs in the examination hall of Trinity College, Dublin. I hope I haven't bored you with this snippet of Irish history, but I feel it is part of our shared history of Ireland and is well worth recording. I counted it a great honour to be a guest in the famous and opulent building, where history has been preserved for posterity. (Wikipedia.... Parliament House Dublin.)

CHAPTER 28

The Moules Marinière

Over the years, we had ten agricultural students from all over the province come to us during their gap year. They were studying for a degree or Higher National Diploma, and their gap year was time taken out from their academic studies to engage in practical work. They were from Greenmount Agricultural College, Antrim. They came to us as boys and left as men. With them being from different and diverse backgrounds, and living with us, we learnt a lot from them. Many went on to obtain excellent jobs in the agricultural industry, while some returned to their home farms. They all fitted into our family exceedingly well and were a very useful extension to our farming business. I became used to having strangers in our home when I embarked on a B&B business after the family fled the nest.

A couple of foreign guests arrived with the gift of a bag of fresh mussels and went on their way, but not before saying they would return for an evening meal, which I didn't normally cook for guests. I had never cooked shellfish in my life, so Rick Stein's recipe came to mind. After steaming the mussels for about four minutes, along with the other ingredients, I discarded the unopened mussels. The Sharpes Express potatoes were ready to harvest, and there was crusty bread. The *moules marinière* were ready for the guests upon arrival and were thoroughly relished by everyone.

I enjoyed hosting guests from all over the world, from Balllyjamesduff, to as far afield as Brazil. Many returned several times. They came as strangers and became friends for a lifetime. I heard some scary stories, but I only experienced one mysterious guest who I have already commented on.

CHAPTER 29

Etched in our Memories

When I became a Christian, I forged friendships with soulmates which have stood the test of time. Sadly, two of them have gone to Glory, only Ida remaining my trusted friend. When a few of these friends turned sixty-five, we were able to take advantage of free travel across Ireland, and we soon got on the ball. A hotel was duly booked in Cork, and we set off on a three-day adventure. As we embarked on our journey, one of our team said that the only time she'd seen Cork was on the top of a bottle. Mary entertained us for the entire holiday.

I'm not really interested in crafts and since the others had planned to go by taxi to a well-known supplier of everything '*crafty*' down Limerick way, I decided I'd go in the opposite direction: to Ballymaloe Cookery School in County Cork. I watched Rachael Allen's Cookery Demonstration on RTE National Television with a passion, so I quickly sussed out bus schedules and so forth. However, my friends weren't happy for me to go on my own. Although I am independent, this time I conceded and went along to this amazing collection of all kinds of material and craft kits by the hundreds. I purchased a lovely felt kit of a farm scene of a hen and a rooster, which hasn't adorned my wall yet, as it is still untouched and safely in its box. Oh, for my Scottish guest to come back! The owner from Limerick generously hosted us with soup, wheaten bread and cheese.

On our return journey, we were halfway to Cork, when Ida discovered she'd left her specs behind. Our typically obliging Irish cabbie, retraced his tracks to the shop and lo and behold when Ida removed herself from the back seat, the *'prodigal'* specs appeared from below her. Patrick, our taxi driver, chuckled: *"The Last of the Summer Wine wouldn't be in it,"* he said.

Lorna Waring, our minister's wife, knew a group of women from the Crescent Church in Belfast who had gone to the *Women's Bible Conference* around Easter, at Capernwray Hall, and had been greatly inspired. On her recommendation we decided to go, as our wee group felt we needed to get topped up spiritually. We joined the Crescent group at the ferry terminal and set off with wonderful anticipation, and I can tell you we were not disappointed.

The following information about Capernwray Hall is taken from the Capernwray website:

'Capernwray Hall is a former country house situated three miles northeast of Carnforth, Lancashire, England. It has a great history. George Marton, who owned the house, represented Lancashire in parliament for ten years and was high sheriff of the county in 1858. He added to the estate with the purchase of Borwick Hall and also built the family chapel in the park. Following his death, his son, a third George Marton enjoyed a time of prosperity at Capernwray Hall and again added to the building. He also arranged for the building of Borwick Railway Station to facilitate freighting farm produce, as well as racehorses to Epsom. Edwin Sharpe was the architect of the House, and in about 1820, it became the stately home of the Marton Family, built at that time for a family of five with thirty servants. The whole estate was much larger than just Capernwray Hall, and comprised some twenty-seven or so farms in the area, plus Borwick Hall just down the road. A fourth George Marton witnessed the decline of the family prosperity, and no Martons lived at the hall after 1939. During the Second World War, children from the Ripley Hospital Trust occupied the premises.

Around the same time, Major Ian Thomas, who was serving with the British Army in Germany, was longing for a place where young people could not only come for a good holiday, but somewhere they could clearly hear the claims of the Lord Jesus in their lives. He sent a telegram to his wife and asked her to go and bid for Capernwray Hall at the auction. On the day of the auction, a reluctant Mrs Joan Thomas went into the town hall in Lancaster, little knowing or realising the full significance that day would have for her, her family, and for thousands of people from around the world. The successful purchase of Capernwray meant that Major and Mrs Thomas could begin to see fulfilled what they believed was God's new purpose for the property — to make it a place where people could come and stay and be introduced to the Lord Jesus Christ.

The first ten guests from Britain arrived in May 1947, and since then many thousands have passed through Capernwray's doors. Now each year 250 students from thirty countries come to the winter and spring courses to study the Bible. Capernwray still continues to offer holidays throughout the year, catering for a mixed-age range of young people, families and a cross-section of adults from around the United Kingdom and from overseas. The on-going aim of Capernwray and the staff involved in the variety of programmes, is to give people from all walks of life the opportunity to hear the life-transforming message of JESUS and to deepen their relationship with Him.' [28]

The website also includes the following words: *'Capernwray offers a unique environment where you can discover, develop or reignite a living relationship with the Lord Jesus through biblical teaching and practical training. Our aim is to equip you so that you leave ready for service in the worldwide church through experiencing the transformative life of Christ working in and through you.'*

For us humble souls from a small rural church in Ballyrashane, near Coleraine in Northern Ireland, the Capernwray experience was one which we will never forget, not to mention Mary taking the stage to dance the Highland Fling for the social evening. You had to be there and see it to believe it.

[28] https://capernwray.org/about/our-story/

Corrymeela Knocklayde, Stroan Road, Armoy is a branch of Corrymeela, bequeathed by an English couple. That was our destination for a weekend retreat for me and my three friends. The *'house parents'* came from Canada to give two years of their lives as volunteers to Corrymeela. The husband, a Catholic from West Belfast and his wife, a Mennonite from Canada, reflected the aim of Corrymeela, where people of all ages and Christian traditions, individually and together are committed to the healing of social, religious and political divisions that exist in Northern Ireland and throughout the world.

Corrymeela is situated on the splendid North Antrim coast a short distance from the seaside town of Ballycastle. But it displays a far greater view than that of its surroundings for the thousands of people who visit the centre each year. In its unique atmosphere of love, understanding, trust and prayerfulness, mutual hostilities and suspicions melt away. The founder was Reverend Ray Davey, a former chaplain at Queen's University, Belfast. Ray was the brother of Dr John Davey, who married us in Aghadowey Presbyterian Church in 1968. Dr John Davey, an ex-moderator of the Presbyterian Church in Ireland, was a saintly man and I was absorbed by his reflections on his thirty years as a missionary in India. His practical and humble Christianity impressed me and whetted my appetite for all things spiritual. When out at local licenced restaurants, he often ended up driving someone home who had over indulged, giving them a tract to read in the morning. He and his lovely wife (a GP) invited a neighbour who was renowned for his problem with a dependency on alcohol, to the manse for Christmas Dinner. The Davey brothers were brought up in the manse in Dunmurry, some miles from Belfast.

The Corrymeela formula of worship declares: *'We are a community of the Holy Spirit. And we pray together. Spirit of the living God fall afresh on me. Spirit of the living God fall afresh on me. Break me, melt me, mould me, fill me. Spirit of the living God, fall afresh on me.'* [29]

---

[29] Taken from Rev Rae Davey's book 'Corrymeela'.

And in the Prayer Guide they use the following prayer:

> *We commit ourselves to each other … in joy and sorrow.*

> *We commit ourselves to all who share our belief in reconciliation … to support and stand by them.*

> *We commit ourselves to the way of peace … in thought and deed.*

> *We commit ourselves to You as our Guide and Friend.*

Corrymeela[30] does not see itself as an alternative church. Most are active members of their denominations. We came away looking at our lives with a different perspective, acknowledging Christ as Lord over *all* our lives, both in the private and public sectors. We recognised that in our loyalty to Him, we resolved to reach out to the hungry, the thirsty, the stranger, the sick and the prisoners. We also knew that above all we had to show forgiveness and the love of God.

I think Corrymeela will be etched in our memories as a place where all identities, like Capernwray, were put into perspective and we were reminded that we are all children of God, remembering afresh His love for us which sets us free and makes it possible for us to set each other free.

The parting hymn by St Francis says it all:

> *'Lord, make me a channel of Your peace.*

> *For it is in giving that we receive,*

> *It is in pardoning that we are pardoned,*

> *It is in dying that we are born to eternal life.'*

We enjoyed many more short breaks across the land and in Donegal.

---

[30] Extracts taken from Rev. Ray Davey's book 'Corrymeela'.

CHAPTER 30

Ballyrashane Presbyterian Church

everend William James Waring, his wife Lorna and their family, Philip, Stephanie and Michael were welcomed to Ballyrashane in 1990, to begin a new era in the life of Ballyrashane. Jim, as he was known, came from Christ Church, Dundonald. Prior to this, he and Lorna served as missionaries in Jamaica for four and a half years, from 1972 to 1976. He proved to be a faithful pastor and was held in high esteem by everyone. It was a new chapter in the history of Ballyrashane when the seventeenth-century church was reopened after extensive renovations, including a building to link the church to the halls. The moderator of the General Assembly, Dr John Dunlop and Reverend David McIlwrath, moderator of Coleraine Presbytery, were welcomed by Reverend Waring, who thanked Almighty God for all that He enabled the congregation of Ballyrashane to do for His Glory. The services were held in the new hall while the renovations were carried out. Lorna was a good helpmeet and led the Presbyterian Women's Association (PWA) until her failing health prevented her from doing so.

It was while Mr Waring was in Ballyrashane that he introduced me to Torch Trust for the Blind. In my B&B I also hosted the Northern Ireland Torch Trust networkers Cecil Bingham and his wife Renee, who are still my good friends. They had a Torch Trust stand at New Horizon, Coleraine. Torch is a Christian organisation which has many resources for the visually impaired. Our first prayer meeting, organised by the

Binghams, to gauge if we could form a fellowship group in the area, was held in Portstewart Baptist Church. After a year, we stepped out in faith and the inaugural meeting was held in February 2002. The VIPs who attended were visually impaired people, but *very important* people in our eyes and in God's eyes too. I was part of the group for nearly twenty years, until the onset of my husband's illness, when I had to resign. I have remained good friends with many whom I got to know through Torch.

I went on a sponsored walk, blindfolded, on Castlerock Beach, guided by Winnie Kelso, a sighted member of the fellowship group. It was a strange sensation; I almost felt that Winnie was pulling me towards the sea.

In aid of Torch Trust, I abseiled from the Europa Hotel in Belfast; it was a tad scary. It was fifty-one metres high. During *The Troubles*, the hotel was where most of the journalists covering *The Trouble*s had stayed. It was known as the most bombed hotel in Europe; hence it earned the nickname *Hardboard Hotel*.

When Willowbrook, in Millburn Road, Coleraine was built in 2001, Philip Waring, the son of our pastor, secured a place there. Willowbrook was an innovative housing scheme, built to support people with special needs. His dad and his mum asked Ida Cairns and me to become Friends of Willowbrook to befriend the tenants and participate in devotions and outings with them. Like the Torch Trust group, they are adorable and so resilient in the accepting of their disabilities.

Sadly, Lorna died in Freeman Hospital, Newcastle on the 11th of August 1999, after unsuccessful heart transplant surgery. This tribute[31] was read in church the following Sunday:

BALLYRASHANE PRESBYTERIAN ASSOCIATION

LORNA WARING

PWA PRESIDENT 1990 - 1999

---

[31] Taken from a tribute to Lorna after her death which was submitted to Wider World Magazine ôf the Presbyterian in Ireland.

'These past days have been difficult ones for the church family in Ballyrashane since the passing of Lorna Waring. We in the PWA have lost a dear friend, but no one will miss her more than her beloved family at the manse, so it is to Mr Waring, Philip, Stephanie and Michael that we extend our love and prayers in these days.

Since coming to Ballyrashane over nine years ago, Lorna has been our much-esteemed president in whom she put her trust; she loved the PWA and each member was equally important to her and in turn they had all grown to love her dearly.

Lorna possessed great organisational skills and was meticulous in her preparation meetings. Her wise counsel was always welcome and many of us have of her memoires inspiring and sometimes challenging words, which were often written from her sick bed. She carried with her the fragrance of the One in whom she put her trust and in her unobtrusive manner, she had a profound impact on many people. Lorna had many attributes which were evident in her church and family life - warmth, affection, reserve, sensitivity, wit, instinctive sympathy, empathy, thoughtfulness, generosity, kindness, resilience, an unswerving faith and most of all a courage which enabled her to allow God to have His way in her life, accepting the rough road along with the smooth one, as He moulded Lorna into the person whom we all grew to love.

Lorna Waring was a supreme witness for God, facing her illness bravely, and clinging onto life, which many of us take for granted, with gentle refinement and grace of manner that marked her entire life.

Lorna's ministry was a wonderful one which was not revealed in great world-shaking deeds, but in those small nameless acts of love that constitute the best points of a person's life. Her humility made her a special person and we in Ballyrashane PWA will never forget her.

The best tribute that we could pay, would be to go forward and build on the firm foundation she has already laid to encourage our members to come to a personal faith in Jesus Christ.

We thank Almighty God for Lorna's witness and for all the precious memories.'

By Diana McClelland

Chapter 31

The Dreaded Phone Call

It was a cold, wet Wednesday morning in November 1999, when we set off for Aberdeenshire to visit our young granddaughter, Grace. We were only there a day when the dreaded phone call came. Ross, our son, called us to say that Ruth had been involved in a serious road traffic accident outside Cookstown and advised us that we should return home. The ferry was booked for the early sailing on Thursday morning, and the five-hour journey through torrential rain to Stranraer Dumfriesshire was stressful and was impacted by our concern for Ruth. There was little motivation to talk to each other. When we arrived at the terminal, I phoned Mid Ulster Hospital in Magherafelt to make inquiries. There were no mobile phones in those days. I spoke to the ward sister, who informed me that Ruth was enroute to the Royal Victoria Hospital. On further inquiring about her condition he replied, *"Do you know that she is in quite a mess?"* That statement almost paralysed me!

We went straight to the Royal Victoria Hospital, Belfast, where we waited an hour to see our precious daughter wheeled up to us on a trolley. Her face was heavily bandaged, as was her body — she almost resembled a mummy! Our fears were somewhat allayed when she uttered a few words of apology for spoiling our holiday! We realised her brain was okay, although she had multiple fractures to her body. After her dislocated hip was put in place, she still suffered excruciating pain, and on the discovery of fragments of bone shards remaining in her hip socket, they had to operate and dislocate her hip again.

I stayed two nights at the hospital while Norman returned home. He told me later, that he had to pull over to the hard shoulder of the road to regain his composure. He was a broken soul and he visited Ruth every single day for six weeks while she was in the Royal.

Ruth was still in hospital when our granddaughter Grace from Scotland, was baptised in Ballyrashane Presbyterian Church. It was a difficult day all round as Norman welcomed our Scottish guests and made reference to Ruth in hospital, it was a rather poignant moment for everyone present. Our very kind friend Renee offered to stay with Ruth in the Royal during the day of the celebration. After exceptional medical care for six weeks, she was discharged in a wheelchair to Tullans. What a resilient girl she was, wrapping her broken leg in a bin bag to shower herself! Just before Christmas she asked me to take her to Coleraine in her wheelchair to buy a present for her little niece in Scotland. Ruth had just entered the third year of her *Food Technology Degree Course* at Loughry.

She had to discontinue her studies until after Easter, six months after her accident. On Easter Sunday, for the first time since her accident in November, Ruth decided to drive our car to the end of the lane and successfully completed the task. Then she asked me to take her to the Moneymore breakers yard to see her wrecked car. I was reluctant, to say the least, but I realised she needed closure to her accident. We travelled to Cookstown to view the wreckage of her car, whose roof had been cut off by the fire brigade to free her.

After graduating with an Honours Degree, she obtained a position in Quality Control in a meat plant in Coleraine. For a time, she liaised with farmers regarding procurement of animals for the meat plant. During her student days she worked in an ice-cream van in the summer holidays.

Ruth was a popular girl with the boys, as well as the girls, and enjoyed her social life. Although she was lively and feisty, there was a charitable side to her. She went with a group from Loughry Christian Union to

Tanzania to do humanitarian work for three months and helped to lead Christian Seaside Mission teams for a few summers in Northern Ireland.

When she met the love of her life Ian, and subsequently married him, a dairy farmer who had visited an ice-cream making enterprise in England whilst on holiday with his parents, years before he met Ruth, the subject of ice-cream reared its head again. Ruth thought it was a good idea if she could work from home and utilise some of the milk from the farm. With her qualification in the food sector, she had a good base to work from. Braemar Farm Ice-cream was established 17 years ago and is recognised as a premier award-winning product. Ruth is very innovative in trying new specialities in the summer period and seasonal flavours at Easter and Christmas. She operates from a trailer on the Promenade at Castlerock seafront, where there is good customer parking. She also supplies some retail outlets. The Pollock family has expanded to three boys, Jamie, Sam and Lewis, who were all keen and competitive rugby players for Coleraine Rugby Football Club. That same club where their Grandpa Norman was a keen player in days gone by.

The medics in the Royal warned Ruth that arthritis could develop in her hip from her injuries. However, years went past with no obvious side effects until we were in Belfast one day and I noticed her limping. I mentioned it to her, but she dismissed my concern. Then her husband mentioned it to me and said she was in pain fairly often. In the intervening time before the birth of her third child an x-ray was not an option, so life went on as usual. Again, we were going to Scotland when she told me she was going to a Divine Healing Service on the Sunday evening. On our return she informed me that she was healed and pain free! God had worked a miracle in her hip. Even now, she and four of her friends (called the Castlerockettes), are undertaking a twenty-six-mile marathon hike for a cancer charity in June 2023.

Ruth Pollock is a legend in entrepreneurship and always seems to be willing to develop, advance and organise her enterprise and be motivated to reach the next level in her business! She has been a wonderful daughter to us, as well as being the proprietor of an ice-cream business, a farmer's wife, and a mother to three energetic and always hungry boys! We are justly proud of her success in the ice-cream industry. She is a keen participant in anything organised by the vibrant and hard-working Castlerock Community Association, along with her involvement in First Dunboe Presbyterian Church.

CHAPTER 32

Like it or not, Change is Unavoidable

As I look back on a lifetime of changes, I realise it's inevitable that life brings changes in a variety of ways to each of us. Sometimes for better - and sometimes for worse, as we find ourselves buffeted by life's storms. If my parents, born in the early twentieth century, were to return to our town of Coleraine, they wouldn't recognise most of it and there is much that is still changing. There are new housing estates, supermarkets galore, one-way traffic systems, diversions and potholes, pedestrian precincts, motorways, and out-of-town shopping. Even our churches have changed.

Our children are changing too - growing up, wrapped up in their new world of technology which we grown-ups don't always understand. As aging adults, we are changing too. Often, I find myself going upstairs for something, only to forget what it was I was looking for. Change can be frightening sometimes.

I was born in the forties, before television, penicillin, polio shots, frozen foods, plastic, contact lenses, videos, compact discs and the contraceptive pill. I was born before radar, credit cards, laser beams, ballpoint pens, dishwashers, electric blankets, air conditioning, drip-dry clothes, and before man walked on the Moon. We got married first and then lived together. We thought fast food was what you ate during Lent, a Big Mac was an oversized raincoat and '*crumpet*' was something we had for tea. We existed before househusbands, online-dating and job-sharing, when a meaningful relationship meant getting on with your cousins, and sheltered accommodation was where you waited for a bus. We were here before day-care centres, multiple occupancy and disposable nappies — which are nothing compared to a line of white towelling nappies blowing in the wind. We had never heard of FM radio, word processors, artificial hearts or yoghurt. Hardware meant nuts and bolts and software wasn't a word. Time-sharing meant togetherness, a chip was a small piece of wood or a fried potato. Before 1940, *'Made in China'* meant junk and a stud was something that fastened a collar to a shirt. We didn't have the choice of an americano, cappuccino, mocha, Irish, short black, latte, espresso, café au lait, flat white, or affogato when ordering a coffee. In fact, even instant coffee was unheard of. Grass was mown, coke was kept in the coalhouse, a joint was a piece of meat you had on a Sunday and pot was a receptacle you cooked in. Rock music was a grandmother's lullaby. A gay person was the life and soul of the party, while *Aids* was nothing more than a beauty treatment for someone in trouble. Those of us who were born in the 1940s must be resilient when you think of how the world has changed and how we have had to adjust to it.

As a farmer's wife, I've seen more changes in the farming sector than anywhere else. Agriculture is a volatile industry and I often say that it's the only industry where the farmer must accept the price offered for his products. We hope our grandson Noah will be the fifth generation to farm at Tullans. Family-run farms are part and parcel of a unique social existence. It's easy to take them for granted and forget that farmers possibly represent an ideal role model for a perfect society. Sadly, because of the unpredictable prices for their commodities in recent years, farmers have taken a hit with falling incomes. The result can be seen all over the country, with the average age of full-time farmers getting close to sixty. Many younger men now work off the farm, and only farm in their spare time. Others have scaled up their farming enterprise — some with excellent results, though others with a negative impact on their lifestyle.

Like us, many have diversified into tourism. Either way the family farm still exists. Farmers are custodians of the land which has been handed down through the generations. I'm happy that our son Ian, is following in his father's footsteps maintaining the farm, even to spray the odd dock which rears its head on the farm, as well as running the caravan park, keeping the hedges manicured and ensuring that the honeysuckle along the farm drive is protected so that the campers can enjoy the scent. Farming is very weather dependant; our campers must accept the rain as we get plenty in Northern Ireland, buffeting storms along with the sunshine. I love sunshine; it makes everyone feel better and the world seems a better place. In bright sunny weather, I often notice the campers have a spring in their step, whereas in wet weather their shoulders are drooped, and their mood is low. In Ecclesiasties11:7 we read *'Truly the light is sweet, and a pleasant thing it is for the eyes to behold the sun'* (KJV).

In Matthew 13:43 Jesus speaks of the people in the Kingdom of God shining like the sun. *'Then the righteous will shine like the sun in the Kingdom of their Father'* (NIV). If you inject warmth into a relationship and have a sunny personality, it certainly has a positive effect on others. It's better than going about like zombies most of the time, instead of letting Jesus smile out of our eyes. The sun is two-fold; it can melt butter, but it also can harden clay. Try to be the butter and not the clay. Look happy and pleasant and you will realise the reality of the old hymn: *'There is sunshine in my soul today, more glorious and brighter, than glows in any earthly sky, for Jesus is my Light.'*[32]

Change is unavoidable and comes like the seasons, whether we like it or not. It's sad to see a person who is not prepared to accept change. I know farmers who would not release their farm to their son for fear of losing control. Sometimes, when the father was ready to let go, the son was no longer interested. He had killed any desire that the young lad had in farming. Don't be afraid of change. If God is bringing

---

[32] Sunshine in My Soul, Eliza E. Hewitt (1851–1899).

you into a new season, rejoice and embrace the opportunity. Norman and I were pleased to release our farm responsibilities to our son Ian. Although Norman still played a consultancy role for several years. We must be prepared to release what we have in order to change, or we will die; spiritually, mentally and physically.

Be prepared to hand over what you are holding onto, and put your hand in the hand of God, who never changes. In the Bible, change is mentioned 151 times. Yet we know there is One who never changes: *'For I am the Lord do not change; So, you, O descendants of Jacob, are not destroyed. Ever since the time of your forefathers you have turned away from My decrees and have not kept them. Return to me and I will return to you'* (NIV). This is a wonderful promise. Likewise, Hebrews 13:8 says, *'He is the same yesterday, today and forever.'* The Greek word for *'same'* is *idio* and emphatically states that Jesus Christ is unchangeable – the one Constant in an ever-changing world.

CHAPTER 33

Even Roses Have Thorns

I t would be wrong of me to say that life was always a bed of roses. Weather terms can be applied to our daily lives. I was in Portstewart recently when the waves were pounding over the harbour wall and splashing white foam on to the promenade. The next day I was in the same town, and it was a totally different scene — blues skies and sunshine - peace and tranquillity all around us.

One Friday night at Tullans we experienced a ferocious thunderstorm. A Met Office warning was in place the day before, but nothing could prepare for the potential damage that such a storm could bring. Tree were uprooted and the roof of a shed was blown across the yard. What do we do when the storms of life approach? Those times when everything is straightforward and routine, and then in a split second we find ourselves in a state of utter turmoil. In such times we need an anchor, who is not only our strength and stay, but stronger than life itself. A famous hymn that was inspired by Hebrews 6:19 and adopted by the Boy's Brigade, declares: *"We have an anchor that keeps the soul, steadfast and sure while the billows roll. Fastened to the rock which cannot move, grounded firm and deep in the Saviour's love."* [33]

Storms came to our door, and to our immediate family, on more than one occasion. In the early seventies we received a phone call announcing sad news. Traffic was chaotic on the snowbound roads in County

---

[33] Will Your Anchor Hold in the Storms of Life, Priscilla Jane Owens (1829-1907).

Londonderry as winter hit Ulster with a vengeance, leaving the roads treacherous. It took three hours to clear the runway at Aldergrove Airport. On the main Garvagh to Limavady Road at Glenkeen, a serious accident occurred between a car and a van, leaving two dead and two injured. One of those injured was my older brother Mervyn. He and his colleagues had been travelling to work at the time of the accident and were quickly taken to Roe Valley Hospital. Thankfully, the two survivors escaped serious injury, but were traumatised at the loss of two dear friends.

My brother Mervyn drowned in Spain in August 2008, having only arrived the previous day. My eldest brother, Ivor contracted a debilitating disease, not unlike motor neurone disease, which caused muscle weakness, slurred speech and difficulty swallowing. He sadly passed away in 2016. Jack, my younger brother, died from a brain tumour in 2019. In 2021, my youngest brother, Ronnie, was involved in a serious cycling accident, suffering life threating injuries. Thankfully, he has made a wonderful recovery due to the expertise of the paramedics and air ambulance crew at the scene, and the professional medical teams in the Royal Victoria Hospital, Musgrave Park Hospital in Belfast and indeed the Lord's healing power.

Yes, the Lord certainly helped me through those rough times, and I was able to walk and not faint, as I trusted Him in every situation.

The following appeared in a church magazine,[34] and I want to share it with you. *'I asked for strength … God gave me difficulties to make me strong. I asked for wisdom … and God gave me problems to learn to solve. I asked for courage … and God gave me dangers to overcome. I asked for love … and God gave me troubled people to help. I asked for favours … and God gave me opportunities. I asked for prosperity … and God gave me brain and brawn to work. I received nothing I wanted … I received everything I needed. My prayers have been answered.'*

---

[34] Quote by Hazrat Inayat Khan, 1882-1927.

Many people have come to faith having witnessed Christians going through life's storms with joy and perseverance, a strong testimony of God in their lives. I love to sit with elderly folk, quietly sipping a cup of tea, and listen to them sharing their stories about testing times. You can see by the wrinkles on their faces, which silently confirm their stories, that they have been through much hardship, trials and tribulation. But they are also folk who have met God through the hardships of life and have mellowed and learnt God-given wisdom and strength. Their stories encourage me greatly. Don't ask God to take you out of the fire today, rather, ask Him to give you the grace and strength to walk through the fire with Him.

'The farmer ploughs through the fields of green,
And the blade of the plough is sharp and keen,
But the seed must be sown to bring forth grain,
For nothing is born without suffering and pain,
And God never ploughs in the soul of man,
Without intention and purpose and plan,
So whenever you feel the plough's sharp blade,
Let not your heart be sorely afraid,
For, like the farmer, God chooses a field,
From which he expects an excellent yield,
So rejoice though your heart is broken in two,
God seeks to bring forth a rich harvest in you'.

(Author unknown)

CHAPTER 34

Trouble at the Door

We were about to move into our retirement home at Easter 2008, when I asked Ian to take over the running of the park. By then the third extension was completed, Ian having overseen the project. However, there were a few problems on Good Friday. I was still mainly using a diary for touring park bookings, with a few on the Internet. Late on Good Friday evening, an irate son burst in. Two vans, which had already been booked from County Fermanagh had arrived late and there were no spaces left. What was he to do? Improvised dual-power connections were quickly put in place and everyone was happy, except Ian. *"If this is caravanning, I don't want to know about it,"* was his abrupt response. We'd just moved into our new home that week and I had mislaid the diary. I had somehow over-booked, and Ian was fit to be tied. I recovered the diary a month later. There were many items mislaid in the ensuing weeks. Norman went to a church committee meeting with his pyjama top under his jacket and was puzzled as to why there were no buttons on his sleeve.

I had purchased a 50kg generator to supplement the electricity supply to the park. This kicked in when an extra load was required. It was a noisy necessity. With more and more electric gadgets in the vans, we eventually acquired a three-phase electricity supply which diminished all our problems.

Carrying a business is never void of excitement. We were in bed one night when Ruth came in to tell us that someone had come to our back door saying there was a man running across the park with something shiny under his arm. I immediately thought it was the TV out of the recreation area, but on inspection it was still in place. Norman and Ian rushed down the road in two different directions, but it was to no avail. The next morning, we discovered to our horror that the front window of a touring van had been prised out and stolen. The occupants came from County Down and were unaware of the incident until the police called them to say they were the victims of a crime. All hell broke loose when the owner's wife realised the van was not insured and she laid into her husband like a ton of bricks. The poor man hadn't a foot to stand on; it was far too late. The police reckoned that some opportunist needed the front window of a Ranger caravan and this one fitted the bill.

At this point in time Ian, who was in his fiftieth year, was working hard on the fourth extension to the park which would accommodate eighty additional static vans. He and Jillian make a good team and carry the mantle well. While it is busy in spring and summer, they can switch off from November to February to recharge their batteries for another season.

Sadly, Nigel, a relatively young man, a great helper and friend of Tullans, passed away earlier in 2023. Robert has filled the breach, and he enjoys a good working relationship with Ian. Both Ian and Robert are farmers, so they have a common interest there too. In fact, Ian maintains that Robert has many similarities to his Dad Norman.

Right from the very beginning we had four families[35] from County Armagh, all with young children, stay in our touring park. They all progressed to splendid static vans and are now grandparents with extended families coming to visit. It's lovely that they still remember me and stop for a catch-up when I'm pottering in the garden as they

---

[35] See testimonial by Gale.

pass by. I amaze myself that I still remember their names after more than thirty years. It also gladdens my heart when many of the residents inform me that they are praying *'God's Favour'* on the park.

Our forefathers were not prosperous, but they had the resilience to survive almost any disaster; they built during prosperity and conserved when times were hard. They experienced good times when a farmer could make money, without even trying. They also had the ingenuity to fill gaps in a widening economic market that centuries of subsistence living taught them. Norman recalled that many years ago, his dad sent him and the *'servant man'* to walk cattle to the market in Limavady, some fifteen miles away. I see that ingrained characteristic in the present generation too, albeit they have an easier mode of transporting cattle today.

Ian's schooldays at Coleraine Academical Institution were undistinguished, although he was a very competitive rugby player. That was very evident when his team won the *Medallion Shield*. He decided to leave after his GCSEs to embark on a three-year *Higher National Diploma (HND)* in agriculture at Greenmount Agricultural College. That year we all went to see Coleraine Inst lift the *Schools' Cup* at Ravenhill. Ian having left school, was cheering from the sidelines, and said afterwards he felt he was on the losing team as he had left Inst the previous year.

Ian's middle year was a placement at the McCracken farm in Ballywalter County Down, where there was a very successful dairy enterprise. During his time there, Ian stayed with Don and Evelyn McIvor. He said they treated him like the son they were never blessed to have. Before returning home to farm, like so many young students, Ian decided to go to Australia and New Zealand for a year. On arrival in New Zealand, he was put in charge of 300 dairy cows — he soon had to think on his feet.

It was on Christmas Day when there was a vacant chair at the table, that we missed him most. But the phone rang, and a chirpy voice wished us *Happy Christmas* and assured us that he was having a great time at a barbecue on the beach, while we recorded a temperature of minus five outside.

When he returned home, I witnessed a transformation in him. He both cooked and tidied his room! His appetite had also increased. I gave him two lamb chops one day, *"I would have had six chops presented to me in New Zealand,"* was his response. He quickly transitioned to working under the supervision of his dad and they had a good working relationship, most of the time. It was during Ian's gap year that I felt we should diversify from mixed farming. After a significant downturn in prices the current situation was not sustainable, if Ian was to go into farming full-time.

It was a few months after his return home that he and two friends travelled to the Highland Show in Ingliston, Edinburgh. On the Highland Show website, it states that the event attracts over 1,000 exhibitors, 4,500 head of livestock, and up to 190,000 visitors. It's the premier fixture in Scotland's farming calendar and is held in June each year. It generates over £200 million in business. The show dance tickets were sold out, so he and his mates went to a disco in another part of the city. Ian's Scottish sister-in-law, said if she had known, she would have persuaded him not to go, as it was reputed to be a bad area of the city. That was where Ian met his fate. I took the dreaded phone call from a consultant at the Royal Infirmary in Edinburgh, who said that Ian had been the victim of an assault and was on life support in intensive care. Unfortunately, because Nana Ruby was staying with us after having been discharged from hospital, Norman had to travel to Scotland on his own, not knowing how he would find his dear son.

Again, God was in the situation. Before Norman arrived at the hospital, his cousin, Nancy Calvin phoned me to say she was at the show and had heard about the incident. Because she was a nurse and a relative, she was allowed into the ICU. Ian was unrecognisable, but the good news was that the doctor assured her the CT scan showed that he had no head or chest injuries, even though his four mandibles (cheekbones) had been fractured when his attacker stamped his boot on Ian's face. Our minister at the time, Reverend Jim Waring came to visit me, and I was so conscious of the church family upholding us in prayer that God's peace permeated my whole being. Nancy told me afterwards; she was amazed at how calm I was. It was all from God. A Bible verse, which I memorised many years before, came to my mind that day. Philippians 4:6-7, '*Do not be anxious about anything, but in everything, by prayer and petition, with thanksgiving, present your requests to God. And the peace of God, which transcends all understanding, will guard your hearts and minds in Christ Jesus*' (NIV).

Ian's assailant was caught and at the court hearing he was sentenced to four years imprisonment. Ian didn't hold any grudge against him; he was just grateful his life had been spared. Thankfully, he didn't have to appear in court. After spending two weeks in hospital, Ian returned home to normality, with four metal plates inserted in his jaws.

It was a short time later that Ian met the love of his life, Jillian. At that time Jillian was heading to university in Nottingham, so for four years it was a distant courtship, except during the holidays. They tied the knot in Ballyrashane Presbyterian Church on October the 7th, 2005. They now have two children, Isla and Noah. I am deeply grateful for Ian and his family and appreciate all his hard work on the farm and in the caravan park.

CHAPTER 35

It's Party Time

Scotland has always been a favourite holiday destination for our family, even before our eldest son, David, went to live there nearly thirty years ago. We visited the Highland Show in Ingliston, Edinburgh many times. One visit to Scotland is firmly etched in my mind to this very day. My dad asked me to drive his car to visit the Workman family's farm in Ayrshire. They were good friends who had left Aghadowey some years previously. Dad and Mum were looking forward to the trip and Dad had ensured me that everything was in place. The oil checked, the tyre pressures measured, and the petrol tank filled to the brim. We had a smooth journey over the Irish Sea and, after landing at Stranraer, we headed north to Girvan for lunch.

Upon returning to the car, I noticed a parking ticket on the windscreen. I looked to see if I had parked on a double line, but I was relieved the car was in the proper parking space. I thought there must have been a mistake. After I looked more carefully at the offending ticket, it indicated that the road tax had expired. I was at a loss to know what I could do as it was the beginning of our week's holiday and for my parents such a keenly anticipated one. I spied a police officer and explained my plight. He was reassuring and helpful. *"Don't worry, just put a wee note in the disc holder to say the tax has been applied for and it'll be fine."* I took him at his word and my fears were allayed. But not my Dad's. He didn't let go of the fact that he had overlooked the tax and on the whole journey to Ayrshire he mentioned it with monotonous regularity. For the remainder of our holiday, he kept repeating, *"I can't understand I missed that tax."* I did feel sorry for him, as he had diligently checked everything before our departure, except the tax. In those days you didn't get a reminder that your tax had expired. I think it marred his holiday somewhat.

A special visit to Scotland was to celebrate David's fortieth birthday in 2011. Unbeknown to him, all the plans had been set in motion some time before. He knew he was going to Crieff Hydro Hotel in Perthshire, supposedly with his wife Anna and two daughters, Grace, who was eleven, and Emma, aged ten. From this side of the pond, extra rooms were reserved in Crieff Hydro for the Irish contingency, a minibus was hired, to be driven by our third son, Ross, and the ferry crossing was booked. Norman and I were the last to be picked up. With eight adults and six children, Janet reckoned it was like the *fat-gypsy* wedding outing. The children were well behaved and many of them slept most of the journey, Hannah was six, Ruby was four, Isla was three, Noah and Jamie were two, and the youngest Sam was only ten months old.

Upon our arrival at Stranraer, we all piled into the minibus again, which was ably but briskly driven by Ross along the west coast of Scotland. The Crieff Hydro Hotel was well-equipped for young families both inside and outside, with fun activities for the whole family to enjoy, modern comforts and hotel standards that you don't usually find in a Victorian Hotel. The hotel management were constantly improving the impact of their facilities on the environment and have used their own water supply since the hotel opened in 1868. A second well came into use in 2007, to meet the increased demand.

Obtaining a master key for David's bedroom proved very difficult. In the end, we told the manager about our plan to hide in the birthday boy's bedroom, so eventually he gave us the key. Anna and the girls secretly texted us updates on David's expected arrival time. We were all in various corners of the family bedroom, including the wardrobes.

David entered the crowded room to a loud rapturous welcome he would never forget. It was a lovely family occasion for a three-day weekend of making memories.

Ian was forty on January the 3rd, 2014, which we celebrated on Lusty Beg Island in County Fermanagh. It was a quirky place with seventy-five acres of idyllic woodlands and lakeside landscapes, situated on Lower Lough Erne. Access was only by car and then a quick five-minute trip on the Corloughoroo Ferry, transporting us to the Lusty Beg experience. At that time of year, we had the place virtually to ourselves as it was to be closed the following week after the New Year break. The restaurant offered a good Fermanagh welcome and local produce. The four-star, self-catering lodges were very convenient for families, providing separate living quarters. There was a variety of water and land-based activities as well as nature trails. That weekend was sadly tinged with the sudden passing of Robin McNaul, a long-term tenant in Nana's house and the man who had fitted the kitchen in our new home. However, we were able to return for his funeral the week after.

Two years later, it was Ross's turn to celebrate his fortieth birthday on March the 16th, 2016. The venue was closer to home, but nevertheless most enjoyable. The Gateway Hotel is located on the Inishowen Peninsula, in north-east Donegal on the Wild Atlantic Way and overlooking Lough Swilly. It boasts a twenty-metre pool and spa. There were two large wedding parties during our stay there, one with 300 guests and the other with 200. It was an education to look at the spectacular opulence of both events. Again, the hotel catered well for young families, and despite the chilly March wind, the children had lots to amuse themselves with outside, while the parents sat watching on the benches. We walked the pier in Buncrana a few times.

By the time Ruth's fortieth came on June the 5th, 2018, her dad wasn't able to travel far away, so we had a family gathering in the Brown Trout Restaurant, Aghadowey and a family photograph was taken. It was a few weeks afterwards that some of the family suggested I should take her on a wee break to somewhere nice, as she might feel she had missed out on the usual fortieth birthday celebrations. She didn't feel at all short-changed, but I rang her with the suggestion and asked her to mull it over. In less than ten minutes - I don't think she had time to mull it over - she rang to say that she had contacted her husband's cousin who has an apartment on Lake Maggiore, the second largest lake in Italy, on the south side of the Italian Alps; and she had been offered it for a few days. Lewis, Ruth's youngest boy (4 years old) accompanied us. It turned out to be quite an experience.

We flew into Milan where Ruth hired a car for the hair-raising two-hour journey to our destination in a little village on Lake Maggiore. The day after our arrival, we had an unforgettable car journey up the cork-screw roads, which snaked through the ancient Italian landscape, to visit a little church on the hillside, and soak up the spectacular scenery and panoramic views of Switzerland on the other side of the lake. As we got into the car for our departure downhill, Ruth noticed a sign for *'Diana's Restaurant.'* *"Let's go there,"* she said, so we ascended to an even higher altitude to have an ice cream and coffee. The next day we took an hour-long boat trip on the lake to Isola Bella, which can only be accessed by boat, to see the magnificent baroque palace with its manicured and terraced gardens that slope down to the lake. That was the first time we saw the white peacocks which reside there. It was all too soon when we had to say goodbye to Lake Maggiore.

Ruth decided to leave it as late as possible to top up the hire car with fuel, but as we got nearer to Milan Airport, there was no sign of a petrol station. However, we eventually found one, filled the tank and went on our way with no time to spare. A kind steward ushered us to the front of the line and fast-tracked us for our flight home. This ended a perfect holiday, despite a few hiccups.

The fortieth birthday celebrations were all very different, but we were so pleased that Norman was able to celebrate them all with us. He always enjoyed a party.

Chapter 36

God Calls Us to Have a Missionary Heart

Reverend David Allen was installed as the minister of Ballyrashane Presbyterian Church on Friday, April 6th, 2001, and remained with us for over ten years. He took on the role Dean of Ministry Studies at Union College in Belfast and subsequently progressed to become deputy clerk of the General Assembly of the Presbyterian Church in Ireland.

David had been a city dweller, but soon gleaned knowledge of rural life as the farmers in the congregation shared their knowledge and experiences of farming; this resulted in David setting up a pig enterprise at the manse alongside the sheep. He acquired a sausage-making machine and strings of edible pork delicacies were shared around the congregation.

David was a wonderful pastor, guide and counsellor to the folk in Ballyrashane. Anyone who knows him will attest to his shy demeanour, his quiet wisdom and his unobtrusive manner; a word in season was his mantra. He always went the second mile - no one will ever know just how many people he transported to hospital appointments across the country! He had a large pastoral heart and was a good listener. Moreover, his exposition of God's Word was where he truly excelled. Sunday by Sunday we were presented with a challenge which we could not ignore.

David was an encourager to each person's Christian journey, especially encouraging an active prayer life. David, his wife, Jackie, children John, Rachel and Chloe won many hearts in Ballyrashane.

The Session Clerk, Desi Lyons compiled an apt poem to mark David's 10th Anniversary in Ballyrashane.

'And now friends, we ask you to honour those leaders who work so hard for you, who have been given the responsibility of urging and guiding you along in your obedience. Overwhelm them with appreciation and love' 1 Thessalonians 5:12–13.

Our highly esteemed minister Dr David Allen

For all the folks within the flock.

Ten years have passed, we've taken stock. Please David, don't you feel upset, formalities, well, they are not your pet.

If just at ease to put you so,

I feel the same I'd have you know. Not one to stand and shout and cheer. More likely to tremble and shake with fear.

You came to this parish in two thousand and one. For you and us a new chapter begun. As part of God's plan, you're the thread. He did choose directing and guiding in His tapestry use.

Very quickly adapt to strange places around. And likewise new faces a name could be found in all spheres of work the nettle to grasp. To each more than equal and up for the task.

Arrived with your wife and your family of three. They were children back then now teenagers be. Yet still not a grey hair do you have in sight. Tell us your secret to stave off the white.

Into pigs for a while though production was slow till the herd
was established and started to grow. Procure a quick fortune
attending to swine, just ask any farmer, you run out of time.

Your farming ambitions now gone by the way. The money you're
saving is now buying hay to feed all the bloodstock perhaps with a
chance of a Grand National winner, that's trained at the Manse.

There's a wee man called Hugo who hails from Strabane. He's a
long way to go to count David a fan. He rants on the airwaves most
each and every day and he tells us he loves us as he goes on his way.

A more subtle approach is David's to claim, never seeking the
limelight or milking the fame. So much that he does is just
in God's sight, unknown to most, except for the right.

Sincere and humble in every way as pastor and friend
in all that you say. On equal footing each one we stand.
Compassion and kindness are your command.

With many gifts David, God's blessed you, so His
word to teach that we might grow. The gift to lend a
listening ear, to draw alongside and ease our fear.

What we do here today is of synchronised mind all ages and
gender, but all of one in kind as we join up our feelings
and wrap them with love directed from God's throne.

So David, this gift we would ask you to accept. Don't feel by this
gesture that you're in our debt. It's merely a token from people
who care. As with the Manse family, we just want to share.

In closing our prayer, for your family would be good health and
God's guidance in all things to see. The bond that's between us would
strengthen and grow. David, our pastor, many blessings would know.

By Desi Lyons

David was a visionary and perceived ways of reaching out beyond the confines of Ballyrashane Church. A summer Holiday Bible Club at Ballybogey Community Hall became a regular outreach project. After sixteen years it is still going from strength to strength and welcoming over sixty children every year. A children's club 'Shine' has also been created and takes place every Wednesday night over the winter months. David also engaged with the local Ballyrashane Creamery to arrange a church service there, with employees taking the service. The local Coronation Club also provided an opportunity for outreach, when they donated a generous gift to the Abanna Trip to Uganda in 2007.

Abanna was a Christian based charity set up by Scott Baxter 25 years ago. Scott was so touched by the plight of the children in Uganda that he felt God calling him to the work. He married Fiona (A member of Ballyrashane church) and they have three children.

In August 2007, a team of twenty-four people travelled to Uganda to help build a new classroom block at Christ the King Primary School, a new education project. The church hoped to raise £15,000 for building materials to enable the classroom block to be completed. This initiative was well supported, and the sum far exceeded the initial target.

 Unbelievable poverty is the lot of most Ugandan people. It's difficult to eke out an existence in Uganda's rural areas. Suffering and poverty have abounded there over centuries. Colds develop into pneumonia; women die in childbirth and children die before they learn to walk. Yet the people are surprisingly happy and accept with stoical resignation that life must include daily hardship. In Uganda, more people die from water-related diseases than from AIDS and cancer combined. For the price of a cup of coffee per day, a child can be put through school, with the supply of books and be provided with one meal daily (£20 per month).

A local Northern Ireland charity based in Bangor, County Down, had been raising funds to help children in Africa. Working mainly in Uganda, *Abaana*, which means *'children'* in the Ugandan language, focuses on education, medication and water supplies. It became our chosen charity. Since 1998, the charity has raised over £800,000 through sponsorship from ordinary individuals across Ireland and the rest of the world. With this money *Abaana* has been able to build a medical centre in Kyanja, New Life Homes, six primary schools in the Kampala area, and sponsor over 1,000 children with funding to pay for their education. Government schools in Uganda are very poor, overcrowded and often there is simply no school.

We were overwhelmed by the financial and prayer support the team received from the Ballyrashane congregation. However, our *Abaana* leaders warned us that it was vitally important we realised that the trip was *not* a two-to-four-week adventure. It started the minute we signed up. We were required to have vaccinations, which included polio, tetanus, yellow fever, typhoid, hepatitis A and meningitis. Even when we returned home, we still had to take malaria tablets, as well as give presentations and talk about our trip. The team was required to go through orientation, then, after training modules were completed, the excitement and anticipation built as we prepared for Africa.

The team of twenty-four was made up of people from all walks of life with a wide range of ages and skills, but we had one thing in common - to make a difference to the people in that rural piece of God's earth in Uganda, and to bring light where there was darkness, joy where there was sadness, and hope where there was despair. The team gelled well, enjoyed fun times and benefited greatly from the prayer and Bible studies at the start of each day. Each person chose to do their best to be a team player and there was never any evidence of division.

One of the highlights of the trip was a visit to meet Eric, a boy I sponsored. Against all the odds *Abaana* had arranged a visit to introduce me to my adopted son. The journey took us over a dirt track that seemed never-ending as the minibus trundled along. As we travelled, we met a peasant, who happened to be Eric's father, loading his four jerry cans of water on to his bike. The waterhole was disgusting. When we turned the last corner, we saw the little corrugated tin roof of a tiny abode in the distance. It was Eric's day to meet me. His mum was wearing native dress — a beautiful emerald-green printed cotton. There she was, slightly bowed and with her hands held prayerfully in front of her in the typical Ugandan greeting. Then she knelt before me. *"Thank you, God for Diana,"* she said. We had travelled a good distance along appalling roads to get there, but it was worth it to experience the humility and gratitude of this dear Ugandan woman. She'd never met me before and couldn't communicate very well, but she loved me. As long as I live, I will never forget the joy that I felt in my heart and the tears that flowed from my eyes.

Then suddenly, there was Eric - with his arms wrapped around my leg! I didn't know his exact age, but I thought he was about seven or eight. There he was with his gentle brown eyes looking deeply into mine. Sadly, six years after this trip, Eric, passed away after contracting a fatal disease when he drank water from a contaminated waterhole. I grieved at Eric's passing

During the team's three-week sojourn there were many heart-rending experiences. Our main aim was to help build a school for primary school children to replace the shack that they called school. As our bus arrived, we were welcomed by a loud chorus of smiling children singing their hearts out. One or two were playing with an improvised football and a hoop. The ball was made up of plastic bags squeezed together in a sphere and then tied together with string, and the hoop was the rim of an old bicycle wheel. And we talk about recycling projects!

When we entered the classroom, we were surprised to see the long hard benches the children sat upon. Outstretched on one was a sickly little girl, barely able to raise her wee head — another victim of malaria. We had taken along boiled sweets to distribute, and the wee pets put the wrapped sweets in their mouths — they didn't know to take off the paper. All of the children carried a small mysterious ragged pouch to school, which contained half a pencil, a rubber and a razor blade to sharpen their pencil. It was certainly not in keeping with our health and safety standards back home.

On the morning after our arrival, work commenced on the school project and local men oversaw the job. There was a gigantic metal dish where the concrete was mixed with water, carried constantly in jerry cans. The scaffolding consisted of sturdy branches joined with rope erected precariously along the line of brickwork. We stopped from our toiling during the hottest part of the day for refreshments and recommenced after a short break. The accommodation was basic and adequate, but we were never sure of a constant supply of electricity.

By the time we left for home, Christ the King School was well on its way to completion and as we said our tearful goodbyes, we all reckoned we would never be the same people again when we returned to the Western way of life. In Uganda, the sparsely stocked food shelves were a stark comparison to our over-laden supermarket shelves that groaned under the weight of every commodity under the sun: hundreds of varieties of potato crisps, an enormous quantity of water, clear and sparkling, and endless confectionary.

The trip wasn't all work and no play. We had a wonderful boat trip to the source of the Nile. The boat was emblazoned with Manchester United. It was a shallow boat and just skimmed the water. One of our team kept dabbling his hands in it — only to be reprimanded by the boatmen. Apparently, the Nile was teaming with crocodiles, and we did see some basking on the river banks.

Seeing the plight of the street children was an eye-opener. They were on the streets from a young age and had very poor prospects for a better way of life. However, *Abaana* had gathered many of these children and placed them into the New Life Homes where they were nurtured and kept safe from harm.

On a particular afternoon we arranged a barbecue; the meat duly arrived in jute bags and was barbecued and distributed to the masses. There were big chunks of beef with the bone still in place, but it was thoroughly relished by all.

We had a doctor and a nurse on the team and on another afternoon, they arranged a clinic where many children received malaria prevention medication. Hygiene was unheard of, and the utensils used at the school were only rinsed in dirty water and reused again which is, of course, why disease was so rampant.

Ugandan children are very photogenic and when a camera appeared they all pushed forward and even climbed the trees to be in the picture. They were adorable and kind-hearted. When they were chewing sugar cane they offered us a bite, but obviously for hygiene reasons we couldn't accept. They had nothing material in this world, but they said they had Jesus in their hearts. As they sang choruses so heartily, we didn't doubt that fact.

We as a team had a desire to obey God's commands in John 13:34, '*I was hungry and you gave Me something to eat, I was thirsty and you gave Me something to drink, I was a stranger and you took Me in, I needed clothes and you clothed Me, I was sick and you looked after Me, I was in prison and you came to visit Me*' (NIV). When the disciples asked Christ what he meant, he concluded, '*Whatever you did for one of the least of these brothers of mine, you did it for Me*' (NIV).

On Sundays we went to church in a large, disused cinema where the exuberant worship had to be seen to be believed. As we travelled along the rough road full of potholes and with open sewer trenches on each side, we were humbled by the line of mainly male adults, dressed in dark suits with their Bibles tucked under their arms, as they made their way to church. Upon arrival, we found the large building packed to full capacity; the service lasted almost three hours. There were no inhibitions about dancing in the aisles.

The leaders of the Commonwealth countries meet every two years for the Commonwealth Heads of Government Meeting (CHOGM) hosted by different member countries on a rotating basis. Since 1971, a total of twenty-five meetings have been held. 2007 was the year that Uganda was hosting the meeting, and it was only two months after our visit. We were told that the street children would be collected and imprisoned during the period of the meeting which was attended by Queen Elizabeth. During her tour of Kampala, the corrupt government wanted to portray a better, although not a realistic image, of the country. We were also told that the president of Uganda, who resides in the state palace at Entebbe, had made a new roadway to his palace to accommodate the cavalcade of cars attending his daughter's wedding. So, it was obvious that two extremes co-exist within the country.

For me, going to Uganda was the trip of a lifetime. Several of the team returned multiple times. Unfortunately, circumstances didn't allow my return, but I thank Almighty God that the memories of my time in Uganda are etched on my heart forever.

CHAPTER 37

Saying "Goodbye" to Norman

On January the 2nd, 2005, Norman's life changed dramatically. We were in church on the Sunday evening when he thought he had indigestion. After church we went up to see baby Hannah, Ross and Janet's firstborn, who was just a week old. Janet noticed that Norman wasn't in his usual good form, and that his colour was off, so we came home. I rang Causeway A&E and when I explained his condition to the doctor, he suggested sending an ambulance for him. As we were only five minutes from the hospital, I drove him in. The doctor said we could bypass the waiting room and go straight to the resuscitation ward where there would be a team waiting. After doing all they could with clot buster drugs to help him, Norman suffered a heart attack later that evening. I sat quietly on the sidelines, observing the experienced team swiftly carrying out their duties efficiently. A nurse slipped over to me, despite her busyness, to say how calm I was. She said some patients' relatives go berserk, which doesn't help either the patient or the medical team. Again, I had that peace within, knowing that God was in charge.

Norman was taken to the Royal three days later to have an angioplasty procedure to insert two stents. Stents are tiny devices inserted to hold the artery open and widen it in an area where it has been narrowed by a build-up of plaque. Stenting is a wonderful invention and is a minimally invasive procedure; it is not considered major surgery. The stents can be made of metal mesh, fabric, silicone, or combinations of materials. Stents used for coronary arteries, as was the case for Norman, are made of metal mesh. After a few days in the Royal, he was transferred to Causeway and then back home. Norman recovered really well but had to be careful not to lift anything heavy or engage in any strenuous work for a few weeks. After that he was back to his old self again and working on the farm as usual. He had fainted in church three months prior to his heart attack and when he returned home that day, he had declined any lunch, taking a long walk on his own instead. I wonder what his thoughts were. Around that time, he also had to rest while feeding silage to the cattle. This was all news to me when he did tell me, and I often wonder if those episodes were warnings of a coronary condition.

A number of years after his heart attack, Norman developed Crohn's disease, which is a long-term condition. The main symptoms are diarrhoea, stomach aches and cramping pain. The main treatment is medication, which reduces inflammation, and diet management. The exact cause of the disease is unknown, although it has been linked to things such as genes, problems with the immune system and stress. After many years of treatment, scans and medical visits, a young consultant surgeon suggested Norman could have surgery. Norman thought it was not a good idea at his age, but the young surgeon suggested it would give Norman a better quality of life, even at seventy-plus years. Norman duly consented and the successful abdominal surgery was carried out, despite other consultants having reservations about it. Fourteen inches of his offending small intestine were removed. For around six months, Norman had no pain and enjoyed a stress-free life, but unfortunately the symptoms returned, and the pain and discomfort recurred as he suffered *'flare-ups'* from time to time.

In his early 80's Norman developed prostate cancer and it subsequently turned to metastatic paraganglioma (cancer of the bone). Norman was an amazing patient, always welcoming visitors and inquiring about their wellbeing and never focusing on himself. He adapted positively to a caring team who attended him four times daily and the community nurses' frequent visits, along with the Marie Curie nurse, all of which enabled him to remain happily at home for which he was grateful. During Norman's lengthy illness our family were indispensable and made themselves available at all hours of the day or night.

When Covid hit the country in March 2020, visiting was curtailed and only the medical team, carers and immediate family were permitted. Norman took it in his stride and never contracted the dreaded Covid. Those months in early 2020 were spiritually rewarding for both of us, as we read the Scriptures, prayed together and discussed all things eternal; we had some precious moments together. There were some funny incidents too. I usually sat up until around 10:30 each night, before retiring to my bedroom beside Norman's hospital bed. On gently easing the door open so as not to disturb him, I noticed his eyes opening. He waved at me, beckoning me in beside him for a comforting cuddle and traditional goodnight kiss. There was not much space to manoeuvre! When I went to my own bed in his room, unknown to him, I usually dissolved into tears and many a night my pillow was saturated.

After someone's death, I've heard it said that people have already done a lot of their grieving. I can identify with that; however, there is always that finality that death brings. When someone is terminally ill, as Norman was, and lingers on for weeks, sometimes months, the process of grieving can be silently going on almost unnoticed. Then when the death occurs at last, the grief has already been expressed and the response to the bereavement is gratitude that at last the suffering is over. Don't think harshly of the person whose grief comes before the actual separation. We don't have the choice between a swift call home or being overtaken by cancer. As Norman sat in an armchair after an afternoon on the bowling green, with one short gasp, he passed from the scene of time. The choice isn't ours. Grief can rush in and build up like a great river that has been dammed, until the dam bursts with an awful torrent of emotion. In other cases, grief flows silently and unnoticed for months and there is no bursting of the dam, those reserves of emotion have been drained dry. All I can say is that my experience of God's perfect peace sustained me at every turn of events. However, there was one night, a few weeks before Norman's passing, when I cried out to God, and asked Him how I was going to cope when the end came. From that time on, all my fears were allayed, and the peace of God prevailed in my heart until Norman's final breath. A previously memorised verse came to mind from my memory — Philippians 4:7 *'And the peace of God which transcends all understanding will guard your hearts and your minds in Christ Jesus'* (NIV).

On October the 14th 2000 a week before Norman's death, the Northern Ireland Executive introduced a new 'circuit-breaker' lockdown, and another partial lockdown was put in place. During the March lockdown, I had been happy with the medical teams still being able to come, and while visitors were not allowed, they spoke to him at the bedroom window. His granddaughter Hannah faithfully appeared daily at the bedroom window astride her horse *Flash*.

During the Covid pandemic, the wheels of society had ground to a halt and everyone's lives had been upended and disrupted to some extent. Hundreds of thousands of people became sick; tens of thousands of people died. A robust economy teetered on the brink of disaster. Families planning their futures were told they may lose their jobs and their retirement accounts were vanishing. Many were living in fear of the possible fallout. Sadly, many people during that crisis didn't have an anchor in those turbulent times. It is sobering to realize how quickly things can change. The Bible says, *'Boast not thyself of tomorrow; for thou knowest not what a day may bring forth'* Proverbs 27:1 (KJV).

Norman was called to his homecoming at 6:15 p.m. on Wednesday October the 21st 2020. While everyone around his bed was overcome with grief, I was overcome with peace, and that peace has never left me.

Because of Covid restrictions we had a private interment in Aghadowey Graveyard, and Norman's mortal remains were laid to rest beside my parents' graves. The Reverend Phil Kerr officiated in our home and took his theme, very appropriately, from the 23rd Psalm. He mentioned how Norman had explained the terminology in sheep farming to him on his visits, but he also made the point that Norman served his Shepherd in so many ways, in his duties as church elder and church treasurer for many years and he was sure that Norman had gone to his *eternal reward* in Heaven.

It was a sad farewell as we carried Norman's coffin from Tullans, the place where he was born, a lived and loved all his life, into the waiting hearse on Newmills Road, Coleraine. As we made our way along the Curragh Road alongside the river Bann, a spectacle of God's faithfulness was displayed. The splendid golden autumnal colours of the trees reflected a golden glassy hue on the river, and again peace was restored in my heart as I thought of biblical times when gold was viewed as a blessing from God. As we approached the Ardreagh Road in Aghadowey, a full rainbow appeared in the sky at just the right time. We read in Genesis 9:13, *'I have set my rainbow in the clouds'* (NIV).

On our arrival at Aghadowey, our son-in-law, Ian, who stood behind the shadow of the church, where we exchanged our marriage vows 52 years before, played an emotive rendition of *Amazing Grace* on the bagpipes as Norman was carried by his three sons, David, Ian, and Ross, and my only surviving brother Ronnie, to his final resting place.

When our late Queen Elizabeth was addressing the bereaved families of the September 11 attack, she famously said, *"Grief is the price you pay for love."* Yes, there is a great void that the death of a loved one brings, but I have proved God can fill that void in so many ways. Someone once said, *'Grief never ends, but it changes. It's a passage, not a place to stay. Grief is not a sign of weakness, nor a lack of faith.'* [36]

---

[36] Healing Gift Journal for Bereavement Recovery by Jessie Stillwater.

Tullans is devoid of Norman now, but he has left a wonderful legacy for me and our family, who have always loved and supported me, and I know they will still be my strength and stay in the days to come. In Revelation 21:21 we read: *'The great street of the city was of pure gold, like transparent glass.'* That's what Heaven is like and that's where my dear husband has gone.

I found the weeks after Norman's death very different. Only the immediate family were allowed to visit, and the carers had all gone, so it went from a very busy schedule of caring for my husband along with the team, to nothing. However, I knew I wasn't abandoned. I had wonderful support from my close family and prayer support from an amazing church family. I sometimes took off in the car to the seaside and sat reflecting on the happy times I shared with Norman. One day when there was snow on the ground, but the sun was shining, I headed to Ballycastle, equipped with a hot-water bottle, a book, a picnic and my phone. A walk on the beach is always therapeutic and I found this a useful and proper way to deal with loneliness. I learnt to be alone without feeling lonely.

Didn't Jesus often leave the crowd to be alone with His Father? Because He knew that solitude is essential to spiritual growth and contentment. I always came home from those outings feeling enriched and better equipped to deal with any challenges that life presented to me. In Genesis 32:24 we read, *'When Jacob was left alone; and a man wrestled with him until the breaking of day'* (NIV).

Out of that time alone with God came a man with a new name, a new nature, a new walk and a new future. When people realise that you can enjoy your favourite meal out, a concert or other activity, alone, they are often attracted by your independence and your inner strength. I reject that I cannot live without a certain person in my life. Much as I enjoyed my spouse of fifty-four years, God is the only one I know I can't live without, and He has promised to always be with me. (Hebrews 13:5)

What of Covid now? Increasingly, the effects of Covid and lockdown are now slowly emerging. Cancer cases have gone undiagnosed, heart disease haven't been investigated, children have missed out on their education. Mental ill-health has also sharply increased, the nation has almost been bankrupted by furloughing, waiting lists are at an all-time high with a backlog of more than seven million patients; and millions of GP appointments and surgeries have been postponed or cancelled indefinitely. There has been an increase in non-Covid deaths, i.e., the number of deaths is greater than it would be in normal times, and running at more than 800 per week. The cause of this is still unclear, but Professor Chris Whitty believes that a possible cause could be the thousands of middle-aged people dying of heart conditions that went untreated during the pandemic. Even children may have been affected. There has been an unexplained peak in Streptococcus A infections, with some deaths. Interestingly, Sweden didn't have lockdown and wasn't any worse off than any other nation. In his opening address, the lead lawyer for the UK inquiry said that the potential consequences of lockdown were never considered and claimed that Northern Ireland should have prepared better for the pandemic. However, Nessa Murnaghan KC, also told the UK Covid-19 inquiry that *"substantial efforts had gone into adequately preparing for the pandemic in the face of addressing other significant issues in the health service in the region. The department reiterates its sincere commitment to learning lessons from the devastating impacts of Covid-19. The department again wishes to convey our deepest sympathy to those bereaved during the course of the pandemic."* They can't do or say any more than that.

CHAPTER 38

Prince Philip, Duke of Edinburgh

After the instability of the war years and the drab austerity of peace, Princess Elizabeth's marriage in November 1947 was a ray of hope for the future of Britain. The beautiful twenty-one-year-old princess graciously walked up the aisle on the arm of King George VI to meet the prince she had set her heart on as a young teenager. The twenty-six-year-old bridegroom recently created Duke of Edinburgh by his soon to be father-in-law, the king, waited patiently at the foot of the steps of the altar in Westminster Abbey.

In those days few people had a television and for the few who did, it was still black and white. The recorded highlights would be seen in cinemas afterwards. Money was scarce after the war; however, many citizens contributed their precious ration coupons, and sent the princess a pile of stockings and hand-knitted jumpers to keep the newlyweds warm in one of the coldest winters in living memory. I have referred to that harsh winter of 1947 in chapter six. The wedding day was bitterly cold and drizzly, but it didn't stop millions of people descending on the streets of London. Over 7,000 police officers were on duty, and it was commendable that there were only two incidents.

In Westminster Abbey, there was great anticipation and a cheerful atmosphere. After the drabness of wartime, it was lovely to see the abbey decked out in cherry red and green. In the spring of that year, the great Parisian designer Christian Dior had just launched the highly flattering *'New Look,'* with sloping shoulders, tight waists and mid-calf length skirts. It was lovely to see the 2,000 guests dressed in the height of fashion. Over 2,500 wedding gifts were received, including a 175-piece dinner service from the Chinese leader Chiang Kai-shek, a gold tiara from the Emperor of Ethiopia and a chestnut filly from the Aga Khan to name but a few. Norman Hartnell, the well-known designer, excelled himself. He created a dress inspired by Botticelli's painting of spring, with pearl embroidery, silver threads, sparkling crystal and made of the finest silk. There was only one problem — most silkworms came from Japan, and to many, so soon after the war, this meant they were enemy silkworms. Finally, Chinese silkworms were found at one of England's oldest estates, Lullingstone Castle in Kent, and the material was woven in Dunfermline in Fife, Scotland. The Princess had eight bridesmaids.

Because of wartime austerity the bride and groom knelt on orange boxes covered with pink satin. At exactly 11:30 a.m. Prince Philip placed a ring made of Welsh gold on the princess's finger, beside the platinum and diamond engagement ring made from stones from his mother's tiara. There was a trumpet fanfare as the happy couple emerged from Westminster Abbey to make their way to Buckingham Palace for a sumptuous wedding breakfast. The Grenadier Guards band played while the guests partook of *'filet of sole Mountbatten'* followed by partridge casserole and *'bombe glacée,'* Princess Elizabeth's dessert. The nine-foot, four-tier wedding cake was cut with the Mountbatten sword, a wedding present to the groom from the king.

After being showered with rose petals by the guests, the happy couple made their way to Waterloo Station and on to Broadlands Hampshire, the Mountbatten family seat. They took with them, Susan, the princess's corgi. The couple spent the remainder of their honeymoon in Birkhall, the Queen Mother's retreat in Scotland, which now is occupied by King Charles. The union between the princess and the duke lasted an amazing seventy-three years. For the first few years of marriage, the Duke of Edinburgh continued his naval career, which began at Dartmouth in 1939, where he won the prize for the best cadet, before swiftly rising through the ranks to serve as first lieutenant during the Second World War. In 1952, when Elizabeth became Queen after the death of her father, Prince Philip became her consort, having retired from the Navy in 1951.

When Britain entered the sixties, the world was in turmoil, perhaps on the cusp of another world war. President John F Kennedy was among the world leaders who were welcomed to the palace by Queen Elizabeth and Prince Philip. Within a few years, Kennedy would be dead. However, the royal family was a picture of stability and contentment with Prince Charles born in 1948, Princess Anne in 1950, followed by Prince Andrew in 1960, and finally Prince Edward in 1964. The monarchy was going from strength to strength. By the eighties, the younger royal generation had taken centre stage as the Queen and the Duke welcomed more and more grandchildren into the family. The nineties brought their fair share of dramas, but the Duke helped the Queen through the bleakest period of her reign.

Their much-loved home, Windsor Castle was badly damaged by a ferocious fire in 1992. It was a sad sight to see our monarch in her welly boots, raincoat and headscarf wandering around the grounds of Windsor Castle to survey the damage. The Duke led the restoration operation and it was completed ahead of time and under budget and was left in a better state than before the fire. In 1997, the Queen and the Duke said farewell to the Royal Yacht *Britannia* and bid a poignant farewell to Princess Diana. Queen Elizabeth's *'annus horribilis'* that was 1992, has become legendary since she described it as such during a speech at the Guildhall to mark the fortieth anniversary of her accession in November of that year. On a happier note, the royal couple celebrated their golden wedding anniversary and marked the historical event at the Millennium Dome on the 31st of December 1999.

The twenty-first century brought both renewal and sadness, yet the royal family rebounded. The deaths of Princess Margaret and the

Queen Mother had a profound effect on the Queen's resilience. The Duke embraced the digital era with great enthusiasm and he was fascinated with the Internet. Apparently, the Queen was often heard to say, *"Oh, I must get Philip to Google that."* There were historic state visits — including one to Ireland. Within a few years, world leaders coming to Britain would sample the result of another of the Duke's bright ideas — Windsor Castle's very own sparkling wine.

Prince Philip spent his final peaceful days at Windsor Castle, and apparently, he retained his sense of humour to the end. Knowing his father had impaired hearing, Charles repeated a remark to him more loudly, *"We're talking about your birthday, and whether there is going to be a reception."* *"Well, I've got to be alive for it, haven't I?"* replied the duke. It was on April the 9th, 2021, that the Duke of Edinburgh's earthly life came to an end, two months before his 100th birthday. *"It was just like someone took him by the hand and off he went,"* said Sophie Wessex. The Queen was at his bedside when he died. The death certificate, certified by Sir Hugh Thomas, head of the Royal Medical Household, stated the cause of death as *'old age.'*

Grand royal funerals are rare occurrences, but the Duke's funeral was like no other ever witnessed before in the history of the monarchy. There were unprecedented limitations placed upon it, as the nation coped with the worst public health crisis for many generations. Sadly, the coronavirus dictated a very different funeral to what would normally have been a spectacular event in the nation's history. The guest list could not exceed thirty people and every member of the congregation wore masks and had to be seated two metres apart.

On Saturday April the 17th, at 2:40 p.m., the coffin emerged from the State entrance of Windsor Castle. The crunch of gravel could be heard as eight Grenadier Guards moved forward in perfect step to perform the unenviable task of moving the Duke's coffin on to the Land Rover hearse. Gleaming in the sunshine, the green Land Rover TD5 130 had been modified to the Duke's own specifications and was only completed when he was ninety-eight. The Duke's cap, gloves and whip were placed on the empty seat of his driving carriage, which was pulled by his two Fell ponies. There was also the red pot that he used to store sugar lumps, which he always took with him to feed the ponies after a driving session.

The coffin was draped with the Duke's twelve-foot personal standard, which featured blue lions and red hearts on a yellow background, representing Denmark and the arms of the City of Edinburgh on four quarters. The coffin was also adorned with a white wreath of spring flowers selected by the Queen, with a private message attached, and the Duke's Admiral of the Fleet naval cap and sword. In moving scenes, the Queen was seen sitting entirely alone in the wooden pew of St George's Chapel. The funeral service, which included hymns and readings, was planned by the Duke and lasted about fifty minutes. One of the readings was from John 11:25–26, *'I am the resurrection and the life, saith the Lord: he that believeth in me, though he were dead, yet shall he live; whosoever liveth and believeth in Me shall never die.'*

Husband, consort, father, grandfather, a military man of strong character, and a man who never liked a fuss, the Duke's decades of service to Britain and his commitment to royal duty have been heralded as exemplary and his kindness, humour and humanity will never be forgotten by the nation.

CHAPTER 39

Queen Elizabeth II

My daughter Ruth and I were sitting watching evening TV News at 6 o'clock on Thursday September the 8th 2022 when the TV screen went black, the National Anthem began to play and the newscaster, who had donned a black tie, announced the passing of our beloved Queen. Our hearts broke as we embraced each other in that moment, as it almost felt that a close relative had died. Elizabeth Alexandra Mary, officially Queen Elizabeth II, *by the Grace of God*, of the United Kingdom of Great Britain and Northern Ireland, Head of the Commonwealth, Defender of the Faith, died at Balmoral, in Scotland.

Just two days previously, the newly elected Prime Minister Liz Truss, who later hailed the Queen as *'The spirit of Britain'*, had an audience with the Queen, who was leaning heavily on a stick. On the morning of the 8th, few, if any, at Balmoral were aware of the momentous events unfolding as the Queen's long life quietly ebbed away.

A minute before the death was announced, a full rainbow appeared over Buckingham Palace, reminding me of the appearance of the rainbow on the day of Norman's funeral two years earlier. *Operation London Bridge* was set in motion and plans that included her state funeral were supported by *Operation Unicorn*, which set protocols for her death that had occurred in Scotland. The United Kingdom observed a national mourning period of ten days and a public holiday on the day of the funeral on September the 19th. The Queen's lying in State took place in Westminster Hall from September 14th to the 19th. The funeral service was held in Westminster Abbey on September the 19th, at 11 a.m. and was followed by a procession to Wellington Arch that featured around 3,000 military personnel. It was watched by around one million people in London. The state hearse then transported the Queen's coffin to Windsor. This was followed by another procession through Windsor Great Park and a committal service at St George's Chapel.

The most poignant part of the service for me, was the ceremonial breaking of the white staff, signifying the end of the Lord Chamberlain's service to the Queen as sovereign. Before the committal of the late monarch to the Royal Vault beneath the floor of St George's chapel, the Imperial State crown, orb and sceptre, were removed from the Queen's coffin and placed on the altar of St George's Chapel, separating the Queen from her crown for the last time. As the final hymn was sung, King Charles stepped forward and placed the Grenadier Guards' Queen's Company Camp Colours (a smaller version of the Royal Standard of the Regiment) on the coffin. The Queen was buried with this.

Queen Elizabeth was interred with her beloved husband Prince Philip, in the King George VI Memorial Chapel later that evening in a private family service. Her death certificate stated that the Queen died of *old age*, as did her husband.

Huge crowds gathered at Buckingham Palace and thousands of floral tributes were laid outside all the royal residences. Our son David was honoured and privileged to be invited to the thanksgiving service in St Giles' Cathedral in Edinburgh. The Royal Family is like a sturdy oak, with branches, but the trunk endures.

History was made when Queen Elizabeth and Prince Philip made their first visit to Ireland in May 2011, and what a warm welcome they received. *'Céad mile fáilte'*, as the Irish President, Mary McAleese explained at the State banquet, was Gaelic for *'one hundred thousand welcomes.'* The admiration for the Queen in the Republic seemed to grow when the people saw her determination as she pressed ahead with a full itinerary at the age of eight-five. The legendary Royal photographer, Arthur Edwards, saw the warm reception given to Prince Charles in Dublin in 1995, and regretted there was no chance for crowds on that visit. *"On a world tour it's the cheering crowds that make it and I know that most Irish people would give the Queen a massive welcome,"* he said. As the trip continued, evidence began to build up in support of Mr Edwards' instincts. At one point, while meeting the stars on the stage, the Queen turned to the crowd who roared back, in what became a five-minute ovation. She seemed startled at the force of the cheer, then touched Mr Edwards, ever present to catch the moment in pictures, and there was moisture in her eyes.

The small crowd who met her at Trinity College in Dublin were plainly delighted. It was on the Thursday night, at the convention centre, that the Monarch got the Irish welcome that so touched her grandfather, King George VI in 1911, and her great-great grandmother Queen Victoria in the 1800s. The Queen and the Duke paid a visit to the Irish Nation Stud and Gardens, forty-five miles from Dublin in County Kildare, to unveil a sculpture. She then travelled to Cork, where a more relaxed security atmosphere allowed crowds to gather and display that *'céad mile fáilte'* and where she visited the famous English Market. There were 25,000 spectators lining the streets of Cork, when the Queen decided on the spur of the moment to *'walkabout'* and meet the ordinary people of Ireland.

It was encouraging to note that the polls taken before the Queen's visit showed that the great majority of the Republic's four and half million population in 2020 — at least three people in four — supported the royal visit. Taoiseach, Enda Kenny, seized the opportunity to repay the Queen's personal touch by inviting her and the Duke to return again one day. Buckingham Palace and the Irish Government were highly impressed by the unprecedented success of the four-day visit, which had seen repeated and deeply poignant reconciliation. I think the Queen warmed the hearts of everyone across Ireland.

My seventieth birthday coincided with the Queen's ninetieth birthday and so Ruth treated me to a few days in Windsor in May 2016, to get the flavour of the celebrations. Every shop in Windsor was festooned with bunting and our hotel was just across the road from Windsor Castle. The highlight was meant to be a visit to see the Royal Windsor Horse Show, but the tickets were sold out in a few minutes, after sales went online months earlier. On the morning of the show, not to be outdone, Ruth suggested we should go to the ticket office to enquire about cancellations, but it was to no avail. Displaying her disappointment along with her Irish charm, she said, *"Oh dear, and we came all the way from Northern Ireland to see the show."* With a wry smile he retorted, *"My dear, there are people here from all over the world, but I'll take your phone number anyway."* At 3.30 in the afternoon of the evening show, her phone rang. *"Hello, Ruth, just to let you know that two seats have been cancelled."* We couldn't believe our good fortune when we were placed two rows from the front of the arena. This is a prestigious show where the world's best horse and rider combinations go head-to-head in show jumping and dressage competitions, providing an exhilarating range of action, right down to the amazing horse whisperer. Many countries' equestrian teams were showcased for this special occasion. We had a magnificent view of most members of the royal family, including Her Majesty, as they passed by before our very eyes in their coaches. Anne, the Princess Royal, followed on horseback.

A visit to Windsor wouldn't have been complete without crossing the Thames Bridge to Eton while hundreds of swans swam underneath. The decorum was significant as the pupils of Eton College, with their files tucked under their arms, stepped off the footpath to let us pass. Apparently, Eton College is a charity for the advancement of education. At its heart sits an independent boys' boarding school which leads a dynamic range of activities and an expanding network of educational partnerships. The charity's primary purpose, determined from its Christian foundation in 1440, is to draw out the best of young people's talents and enable them to flourish and make a positive impact on others through the course of a healthy, happy and fulfilling life. Famous alumni of Eton include Boris

Johnston, David Cameron and Harold McMillan. In total twenty British prime ministers went to Eton. The Royal family also sent members to the school over the years including Prince William and Prince Harry. After coming down to earth again, we proceeded to a posh café for scones, strawberry jam and clotted cream, followed by a visit to the Windsor farm shop where we treated ourselves to the proverbial ice cream. *'Making memories'* couldn't encapsulate our Windsor experience.

Another seventieth birthday treat took me to Vilamoura, in the Algarve in Portugal. Jillian, my daughter-in-law had scanned my passport, and everything was in order, or so I thought, until I was at the check-in at the International Airport. As I produced my passport, two loose pages fell to the floor and upon inspection, the attendant said I couldn't fly. Then she changed her mind and said I could proceed, but she couldn't guarantee my return from Portugal. On discussing the faulty passport, I suggested I could stick the pages in with Sellotape, but Jillian that might be considered as tampering. Then Noah came up with the bright idea of giving me the plastic holder off his passport. After five enjoyable and relaxing days in the Algarve, we were confidently homeward bound. When the attendant at the check-in took my passport out of its sleeve, the pages fell to the floor again. The problem was that my photo was on one of them. She shrugged her shoulders. *"Those bloomin' holders are a proper nuisance, that happens all the time,"* she said and happily returned the passport to me. But worse was to come when I was stopped at security and relegated to the side of the booth, to await approval. Jillian, Isla and Noah all went through security, awaiting *'yours truly'*, who remained standing like a criminal as dozens of holidaymakers filed past. Poor wee Noah looked worried as he supposed I was surely destined to stay put while they returned home. The attendant with my passport in one hand and phone in the other hand, pranced from ticket booth to ticket booth with a stern and negative look on his face, accompanied by the continuous shake of his head. Eventually, with very little time to spare, he gave me a nod of approval. I could have kissed him. The mystery remained unsolved, and a new passport was purchased for my next trip. Hallelujah!

CHAPTER 40

The Coronation of King Charles III

t was in January 2023, when I booked a coach trip in June to Skegness, with day tours to Lincoln and Sandringham in Norfolk. As the months passed, I was anticipating a lovely holiday with my two friends, when I received a phone call from my daughter Ruth. *"Hey Mum, Janet and Jillian and I are thinking of going to the Coronation in May, would you like to go with us?"* I said I wasn't sure if a septuagenarian could keep up with them in the streets of London. *"You have ten minutes to make up your mind, the prices are increasing by the minute,"* she replied. I decided quickly and called her back with a resounding *"Yes!"* and the die was cast.

The Coronation of Charles III and his wife Camilla, as king and queen of the United Kingdom and the other Commonwealth realms, was to take place on Saturday, May the 6th, 2023, at Westminster Abbey. Charles had acceded to the throne on September the 8th, 2022, upon the death of his mother.

Accommodation was booked in Piccadilly for Friday and Saturday, the 5th and 6th of May. Monday the 8th was declared a public holiday. On the morning of the Coronation, as dawn was breaking at 4:15 a.m. we set off on a quest to get a strategic viewing point on the Mall. We were most certainly not the only spectators to arrive early; there were lots of people milling around. As the sun came up, despite the negative forecast, there was a glimmer of hope, but it soon disappeared to give way to drizzle which continued throughout the day.

We decided to split into pairs and the two girls went up nearer Westminster Abbey, while Ruth and I stayed beside the entrance to Clarence House. They decided to stay put as they were beside a large screen and just two rows from the barriers. We were happy to stay where we were and, as the space that was reserved for the press was not used, we were able to move right up to the barrier. By 8:00 a.m. there were fifteen rows of people behind us, and it was still increasing. Tents had been erected by the hundreds, but people were asked to dismantle them before the procession. Before it began, a convoy of eight limos emerged from Clarence House enroute to Buckingham Palace, probably for a cup of tea before the formalities began. As we engaged with the people and enjoyed the camaraderie around us, I recognised a Northern Ireland accent and sure enough, it turned out to be Lorna, a Methodist minister, whom I had watched online weekly during the pandemic. Beyond her, were three women from Israel who had flown in that morning and were returning in the evening. Over my left shoulder was an elderly lady from New Zealand and to my right, a similarly aged woman from Toronto, both solo travellers, neither were British born, but they had a love for the Royals. The rain fell softly all day, but it didn't dampen our spirits. We had stools and Ruth kindly loaned hers to the elderly woman behind her. The loan lasted around three hours, when a reluctant and timid Ruth finally asked her kindly for its return. The lady had forgotten it was just on loan.

Monarchs have been crowned in the magnificent setting of Westminster Abbey since 1066. The last monarch to make the traditional route to Buckingham Palace from the Tower of London was Charles II, when he was crowned on April the 23rd, 1661, resplendent in the regalia of ermine-trimmed robes, crown, sceptre (a sign of the monarch's spiritual role) and orb (a symbol that the monarch's power is derived from God). These powerful symbols had been destroyed following the execution of Charles II's father, Charles I, and a new set had to be made for Charles II's coronation. The symbolic emblems still played a significant part in the coronation of King Charles III.

Even as an onlooker only, it was a wonderful experience to be on the Mall to witness this historic day. The formal celebrations started with a procession from Buckingham Palace to Westminster Abbey at 10:50 a.m. In a break with tradition, and a nod to the Queen, King Charles and Queen Camilla travelled in the Diamond Jubilee Coach, rather than the old, uncomfortable State Coach. They arrived at the Abbey at 11 a.m. for the commencement of the service at 12 noon, which lasted two hours and was attended by 2,000 guests. King Charles III was crowned by The Archbishop of Canterbury, Justin Welby. The crowds were ecstatic as the royal procession passed by. Around 7,000 personnel were on ceremonial duty, 1,000 of them lined the streets and had to face the crowd, instead of the procession. There were more than 900 personnel from the Royal Navy and Royal Marines — close to 4,000 from the British Army and some 900 from the Royal Air Force, with more than 400 personnel from thirty-nine British Overseas Territories flown in. Each Commonwealth flag was carried on the right shoulder of the army personnel. Nineteen military bands played and were separated by the length of a mile along the procession, and yet had to strike up at the same time, along with maintaining a constant 108-pace beat. Sixty-eight military aircraft from all three services including the Red Arrows, who performed the full Battle of Britain Memorial Flight, took part in a six-minute flypast down the Mall and over Buckingham Palace.

The precision and logistics of the whole operation were mind boggling. As Brigade Major Lieutenant Colonel James Shaw said, *"The Army has been supporting coronations for a thousand years in this country, so we've got plenty of precedence. We're part of that history, it's very exciting. His Majesty, the king is our colonel-in-chief, we have a very strong bond. It's going to be very special for all on parade, and I'm confident we will get it right."* They certainly surpassed all expectations.

In the King's 2022 Christmas address to the nation, he said, *"Some years ago, I was able to fulfil a life-long wish to visit Bethlehem and the Church of the Nativity. There, I went into the Chapel of the Manger and stood in silent reverence by the silver star that is inlaid on the floor and marks the place of our Lord Jesus Christ's birth. It meant more to me than I can possibly express, to stand on that spot where, as the Bible tells us, 'the light that has come into the world, was born.'"* May that same Light that the king spoke of, still spread its shining rays across this world today and always.

On the King and Queen's return down the Mall, all the tents had been taken down and the security barriers had been dismantled with precision; the security staff allowed each section of the crowd to spill on to the Mall. We saw Jillian and Janet, who were behind us at one stage, sprinting along away ahead of us. Each section was stopped for a few minutes and then an orderly surge took place periodically, until we managed to get past the Queen Victoria Memorial and just a few yards from the Palace gates. The other two girls got even closer and were interviewed by a TV reporter. Fifteen members of the Royal family gathered on the balcony of Buckingham Palace to watch the flypast by the British Armed Forces. The drizzle somewhat masked the true effect of the spectacular display, but it was performed with the usual precision.

We four travellers returned home with gladness in our hearts to have been part of a story that will go down in the history books of our nation.

CHAPTER 41

An Amazing Flower Show

Our son David, from Aberdeen, invited me to join him on a trip to Oxford to visit his daughter Emma. He picked me up at Edinburgh Airport and we embarked on our nine-hour car journey heading south. It was most enjoyable as we drove along the M6 between Lancaster and Penrith, through the Lake District and the Yorkshire Dales in brilliant sunshine, stopping off at Tebay Farm Shop and Services, Cumbria - an amazing farm diversification programme, but that's for another day. On arrival in the beautiful ancient city of Oxford, we settled into an Airbnb, and caught up with Emma who took us on a city tour. We were up with the lark the next morning and all three of us set sail to a car park near Heathrow, from where we took the tube into Sloane Square and walked to Chelsea. Each shop doorway was decked with flowers depicting a TV character. What a sight to behold as we savoured the vastness of the Cheslea Flower Show, which is in the grounds of the Chelsea Pensioners Hospital.

On the flight over to Edinburgh, I was seated beside a woman who had been to the Royal Horticulture Society's Chelsea Flower Show three times. She advised us to go early as the coach-loads flock in around 11 a.m. That advice proved invaluable. The show covers more than twenty-three acres with 500 exhibitors and is the highlight of London's summer season. The five-day event, held in May each year, is attended by 157,000 people and is a must-visit to see the *'best of the best'* in cutting-edge garden designs and horticultural exhibits. It is popular with the Royals, and celebrities, as well as professional and amateur gardeners like us.

One of the many award-winning garden designs that year, was a stunning space created by a Samaritan volunteer, to help the charity celebrate seventy years of supporting people struggling to cope with life. Seats were strategically placed in the garden space as a reminder that, while the path to hope can seem full of obstacles, there is always support available. Many aspects of gardening were showcased and provided many new stylish ideas to aid the aspiring gardener.

Following the Chelsea Flower Show, the Samaritan Garden was permanently relocated to Samaritans branches across the UK. In addition, any building materials not able to be repurposed re-entered the recycling process from where they were originally sourced. It was a world-class flower show, and I will remember it as an inspiring experience for years to come. Of course, the glorious sunshine was an added bonus on the day. You, dear reader must pay it a visit.

We spent the following day visiting Blenheim Palace and its extensive gardens. Early in Queen Anne's reign, England became involved in European war — the War of the Spanish Succession. Charles II of Spain died in 1700, and left his vast empire to Prince Philip, grandson of Louis XIV of France, England, Austria and the Netherlands. All these countries feared the idea of a union between France and Spain, as it would make France far too powerful. So, they formed an alliance, and claimed the throne for the Archduke Charles of Austria instead. In 1701, war broke out between the two factions. A young general named John Churchill helped win a series of outstanding victories, and secured England's reputation as a major European power. He became a national hero. Queen Anne rewarded him with the title, Duke of Marlborough, and she gave him a large plot of land, where he built a magnificent palace called Blenheim, named after one of his most famous battles. The Queen and the Duke of Marlborough's wife, who was a courtier named Sarah Churchill, were close friends since childhood. Sarah's influence helped her husband rise to a position of political power and influence. However, when Sarah tried to persuade Anne to put more Whigs into office, Anne resisted. Eventually, the women fell out and the Duke was dismissed from his position in government, despite his popularity and success.

Blenheim is still home to the Churchill family and is currently occupied by the Twelfth Duke of Marlborough. The land is now owned by the King, since the passing of Queen Elizabeth II. The family has paid rent for the lands for the past 300 years. It is the only non-royal house in England to hold the title of palace. With 187 rooms, the palace has a footprint of seven acres. The estate covers over 2,000 acres. The gardens are the work of Capability Brown, who sculpted the vista using the undulating hills and clusters of trees and dammed the river to make the enormous lake. It was at Blenheim Palace on November 30th, 1874, at 1:30 a.m. that Winston Churchill, *'the greatest of all time'* was born. I had the privilege of visiting the bedroom where Sir Winston Churchill was born.

Henley-on–Thames overlooks the Chiltern landscape of wooded hills and green fields and is only twenty miles from Oxford and a short distance away from Blenheim, and it was our next stop, on our way back to Oxford. We had planned to pop in to visit Alan Campbell, the Olympian medallist (and a second cousin of Norman's), in Henley, but he was away with his family for the Bank Holiday weekend. Nevertheless, we had a potter around Henley and enjoyed a meal in The Angel on the Bridge. Henley is a world-renowned centre for rowing and is home to Mary Berry, the food writer and TV presenter. Dusty Springfield, my pop idol as a teenager, is buried in St Mary the Virgin Parish Church. Musician and former Beatle member, George Harrison, lived in Henley until his death in 2001. While travelling north, I couldn't help but think of Norman, who would have enjoyed the scene of massive fields of farmland, as far as the eye could see, not unlike Aberdeenshire, where some of the fields are over 100 acres, almost the size of our whole farm at Tullans. He used to comment that we were only market gardening in Northern Ireland and used to intimate, had he been thirty years younger he would have bought a farm in the north of Scotland. I returned home once again with a thankful heart.

SKEGNESS AND SANDRINGHAM

A fortnight later and the sun was still shining when we set off on a coach tour in the early hours for the east coast of England, to Skegness, which the locals call '*Skeggie*' There is much to visit there; The seal sanctuary, the aquarium and we walked the long pier reaching to the North Sea to see the wind farms. The superb Savoy Hotel was on North Arcade and convenient to all amenities. Whilst there, we made a day trip to the historical city of Lincoln and a visit to the cathedral, a building which was started 940 years ago, and which took 200 years to complete. After the Battle of Hastings in 1066, William the Conqueror instructed the bishop of Lincoln to build the cathedral. A spire was added to the central tower in 1311 and made it the tallest building in the world. In 1348 the black death reached England. The central spire blew down in 1548. In 1644, Cromwell and his soldiers did their damage. Can you imagine boys as young as eight were set to work as stone carvers in the cathedral? The Great Tom bell was lifted into the clock tower, and you can still hear it ringing today. The Father Willis organ was installed in 1898. There is a very special seat called a 'cathedral' and it got its name from the Latin word '*cathedra*' meaning '*seat*'. This is where the bishop sits during services. Our visit began in the nave, a word which means '*ship*'. If you look at the roof, it looks like an upside-down boat. The Magna Carta, sent to Lincoln in 1215, was read out at the sheriff's court in Lincoln Castle, before being placed in the cathedral treasury for safe keeping. It has been retained in Lincoln ever since and is one of only four surviving originals.

Sandringham House was the icing on the cake for me. Again, a lovely sunny day presented it at its best. It is an opulent country house in the Parish of Sandringham, Norfolk, 100 miles from London and is one of the royal residences of King Charles III, whose grandfather, George VI, and great-grandfather George V, both died there. The house stands in a 20,000-acre estate in the Norfolk coast, an Area of Outstanding Natural Beauty (AONB). King George V said of Sandringham, *"Dear old Sandringham, the place I love better than anywhere else in the world."* He died at the house on the 20th of January 1936. The estate passed to his son Edward VIII, but at his abdication, as the private property of a monarch, it was purchased by Edward's brother George VI. George was as devoted to the house as his father. He wrote to his mother Queen Mary: *"I have always been so happy here, I love the place."* He died at Sandringham on the 6th of February 1952. Sandringham House's main floor rooms are used regularly by the Royal family and are open to the public. The décor and contents remain very much as they were in Edwardian times. Both Queen Alexander and Queen Elizabeth were keen collectors of objects *d'art*.

To walk up the steps to St Mary Magdalene Church on the estate evoked fond memories, as I recalled seeing, on television, members of the Royal family ascending and descending those same steps. When they stay at Sandringham, they attend church regularly and especially at Christmas, a poignant reminder of the passing of time. Many royal baptisms have taken place there. King George VI in 1896, Diana, Princess of Wales in1961, Princess Eugenie of York in 1990, Princess Charlotte in 2015, and King Olav V of Norway in 1903, to name but a few. Lady Diana Spencer was born at Park House, a home on the Sandringham Estate. Park House was the family home of Diana's mother, Frances, whose mother was a lady-in-waiting to the Queen Mother.

CHAPTER 42

Ruby Cottage

've heard people say that when they are in the eventide of life, they are in the departure lounge. I have said that myself, but I'm not taking off any time soon.

Bereft of my husband of fifty-two years, I found the retirement home we built fifteen years ago, superfluous to my needs. I was only occupying two rooms as my occasions for entertaining were grinding to a halt, except for family gatherings. So, downsizing was foremost on my mind when I went to view an apartment in Coleraine. However, the more I contemplated the move to urban living, the more intense my thoughts were about how I would miss the rural ambience of Tullans. Then I thought of a log cabin, but that idea was soon quashed and went out the window too.

God had woven His threads through my life even before my conversion in 1983, and this time was no different. It's God who makes things happen, it's His gracious hand that gives and gives and gives again.

It was a sunny autumn morning in 2022, and I was brushing up the fallen leaves when my daughter-in-law Jillian called. *"I hear you are thinking of moving,"* she said. These WhatsApp family groups hold no secrets. That conversation with Jillian was one of those divine moments. *"Why would you want to invest in something when there is a house up in the farmyard?"* she asked. *"But that house is yours and Ian's,"* I replied. *"We've been discussing it and you can have it,"* she said.

Ruby cottage is a stone dwelling, probably erected in the early 1800s, and it has been let to tenants for eighteen years, since Nana's passing. It is structurally sound but needs a wee makeover to spruce it up. It was going to be our temporary home when Norman and I returned from our honeymoon in August 1968, as our new home was slowly being constructed. However, I got along famously with my in-laws, and realised that living with them would not be permanent and that we would have our new abode sometime down the line.

So, in the spring of 2023, I possessed a feel-good factor and my plans for the move were put into action. A new kitchen and bathroom were chosen and gallons of paint were purchased for my relocation to Ruby Cottage. It's now mid-summer and I still haven't moved. Two Canadian relatives of Norman's are coming to stay for two weeks in August, so the transition is on hold until possibly the winter. Don't they say, *'Home is where the heart is?'* God just calls me to be faithful and to nurture the dream He has put in my heart. When the time is right, He will set everything in place.

American Gospel songwriter, Eugene L. Clark, penned one of my favourite songs, *I Know Who the Future*. It was sung at our daughter Ruth's wedding in 2005. Here are the words:

I do not know what lies ahead, the way I cannot see; Yet One stands near to be my guide, He'll show the way to me.

Chorus: I know who holds the future, and He'll guide me with His hand, with God things don't just happen, everything by Him is planned; So as I face tomorrow with its problems large and small, I'll trust the God of miracles, give to Him my all.

I do not know how many days of life are mine to spend; but One who knows and cares for me will keep me to the end.

Chorus.

I do not know the course ahead, what joys and griefs are there; but One is near who fully knows, I'll trust His loving care.

Chorus.

Isn't it lovely that the God of the Universe is always in control of our lives? I am not a Bible basher, but as I encounter cynical people who argue against the God of the Universe, I feel compelled to disagree with them as I face the constant bombardment of comments every time I lift a newspaper or click on my computer. I have a heavy heart for lost souls. This is the anti-God world that has taken hold, all around us. Dear friend, what kind of Bible do you read? In our technological world it could be a leather bound one, a computer monitor, a smartphone, an iPhone or a tablet. While they contain God's Word, like everything today, which we have been given by God, they need to be handled wisely as these devices can be nourishing or toxic. These devices may make people redundant, but they may also make things more efficient as they can spread the good news of the gospel far and wide. In this modern world in which we find ourselves, whether we surf the net or tweet, we need to be wise to do it all to God's Glory as we walk each day with Him.

I thank God that I am driven to share that the God of all hope and peace, whom I love and worship, is the same God who died for me. He sent that precious baby to Bethlehem, over 2,000 years ago. He led Him through childhood to manhood. Jesus, came to do His Father's will and this led Him to the depths of Gethsemane, and to the judgement hall of Calvary. When I was without strength, Christ died for me. When I was godless, Christ died for the ungodly. God loved the church - good. Christ the loved the church - better. But the Son of God loved ME and gave Himself for ME - absolutely supreme. No person was ever born again of the Holy Spirit without first learning the need of Him. Why did the Lord Jesus pick me, Diana McClelland? Why you? Why when millions in this modern age rush on to eternity with absolutely no thought of spiritual things? The Lord Jesus found me in the field as it were. *'The field is the world'* Mark 13:38 (NIV). He gave me spiritual food and drink and set me in His banqueting house and His banner over me is love. Then as if that was not enough, He drops handfuls of purpose and blessing along the way. Why me? My dear reader, if I could answer then I would be God. *'I know not why, I only cry, how He loves me.'*[37]

---

[37] Johnson Oatman, Jr (1856-1922) the Pilot Hymnal.

I am an avid reader of Catherine Marshall's books. I recall reading the story of a dream she had about her husband, Peter. In the dream, she was discussing with him the biography of his life that she was occupied in writing, when he laid down a condition. What was the condition? *"Tell the world, Catherine, that a man can love the Lord and not be a cissy."* [38]

I like it. From young, we are all taught that manliness is all about strength — which usually involves being well built, tough and emotionally impenetrable. Taken one step further is the macho man who is full of bravado. The macho man will try to protect his 'invincible' image and not back down from any confrontation. Contrary to these ideas, Jesus was tender-hearted and in touch with His emotions, as much as he was focused and confident. He did not have an impressive appearance to draw people to Him, yet Jesus was the strongest man ever to walk on earth. His strength came from knowing His identity; that He was the Son of God, and nothing could change that for all eternity. Definitions of what it means to be a man in the world's eyes are totally irrelevant before God. Jesus wasn't a doormat, but He became one, for the sake of others.

Any man who follows Jesus will be challenged by worldly alternatives of what it means to be *'a real man.'* Let me warn you that if we conform to the patterns of the world, we will become less and less like Jesus. Instead, God calls you to be well-trained men who have the courage to follow the example of their eternal male role model, Jesus Christ, who has set His example for you. The choice is yours, all you men.

Many of the people to whom we witness, put on a mask of indifference, but we never know what's churning in their minds. When we seek to live a consistent Christian life, quietly but faithfully praying, and taking opportunities to speak, there can be new openness in time. Before I came to faith, the one thing that put me off, was someone who would *'buttonhole'* me about it. In Isaiah 55:11 we read God's promise, *"So*

---

[38] A Man Called Peter' by Catherine Marshall.

shall My word be that goes forth from My mouth, it shall not return to Me void, but it shall accomplish what I please, and it shall prosper in the thing to which I sent it" (NKJV). It can be an easy mistake to conform our beliefs to current politically correct opinions, but it leads to insipid and lukewarm religion. We should not be bombastic, but loving and winsome, yet we should also be faithful and true to Scripture. We have no right to look down on anyone, no matter how much they have scarred themselves in their fight against the Lord. Our aim is not to win an argument, but to see people coming to a saving faith in Christ. Actually, there are times when we might imagine there is going to be a vibrant conversation, but they have a spiritual hunger which overrides natural antagonism. God in His grace has prepared the way.

I mentioned in a previous chapter how I, as a fledgling Christian, benefited from The Navigators discipleship course. Dawson Trotman, the founder of The Navigators, was a soul-winner and a disciple-maker, whose influence spread throughout the world, as he ministered in Schroon Lake in Upstate New York. Dawson Trotman once said, *"Soul-winners are not soul-winners because of what they know, but because of the person they know, how well they know Him, and how much they long for others to know Him."*

He and Jack Wyrtzen took two teenagers on a lake in a motorboat, but on turning the boat at speed, both young people were thrown out of the boat and into the water. They both cried out, *"I can't swim!"* Trotman dived in to rescue them. He rescued the first and then the other one near the boat, and Wyrtzen pulled each to safety. As Trotman put out his hand to be pulled up, somehow Wyrtzen's grip slipped, and Trotman went under. Wyrtzen said later, *"The whole of the US Navy could not have saved Dawson; his time was up."* Time magazine carried his obituary, and under Trotman's photograph it said, *'Always holding somebody up.'* Isn't that our calling as Christians today? Nothing lifts a person like the Gospel; there is no Saviour other than Jesus, and no way to God than through His forgiveness of sin. The Lord has entrusted to us as Christians, the most valuable service in proclaiming Christ graciously and lovingly, to a lost world, which is without hope because it is without Christ. As I write the last chapter of this book, it is my prayer that I will be obedient to this Heavenly calling to make Christ known and make disciples of Jesus from those who will repent and believe.

I have learnt to rest in God's presence when I need refreshment. Remember resting is not idleness, as people often perceive it. When you rest in God's company, you are demonstrating trust in Him. Trust is a rich word, laden with meaning and direction for your life. Many people turn away from God when they are exhausted, associating Him with duty and diligence, so they try to hide from His presence when they need a break from work. How that must sadden Him. The prophet Isaiah wrote in Chapter 30:15 (AMP), *"For thus said the Lord God, the Holy One of Israel; In returning (to Me) and resting (in Me) you shall be saved; in quietness and in (trusting)confidence shall be your strength."* Over the past few years of widowhood, I've learnt to be alone without being lonely. Jesus often left the crowd to be alone with his Father in prayer. Why? Because He knew that solitude is essential for spiritual growth. And He came back from those times personally enriched and better equipped to deal with the challenges of life.

You and I know that in today's world, we live among people who glorify busyness; they have made time a tyrant that controls their lives. Even those who know the Lord sometimes tend to march to the tempo of the world. They have bought into the illusion that more is always better, more meetings, more programmes and more activity. But God has called believers to follow Him on a solitary path, to make time alone with Him their highest priority and deepest joy. It is a pathway largely unappreciated and often despised by the world. However, like Mary in Luke 10:44, *"But only one thing is needed. Mary has chosen what is better and it will not be taken from her"* (NIV). Moreover, as we walk close to God, He will bless others through us.

Unfortunately, in this day and age, we need to be alert as affluence can creep into all of our lives, and idolatry can be the downfall of many people. God makes no secret of being a jealous God (Exodus 20:4–5). Current idols are more subtle than ancient ones, because today's false gods are outside the field of religion. People, possessions, status and self-aggrandizement are some of the most popular deities today. Beware of bowing down before these things. False gods never satisfy, instead they stir up lust for more and more. When you seek the true God, instead of the world's idols, you experience His joy and peace. These intangibles slake the thirst of your soul and provide deep satisfaction. The glitter of the world is tinny and temporal. The light of His Presence is brilliant and everlasting. Walk in the light with God, thus becoming a beacon through whom others can be drawn to Him.

Don't be afraid to be different from other people. To follow God wholeheartedly, you must relinquish your desire to please other people. The Bible says in Matthew 12:30, *"He who is not with Me is against Me, and he who does not gather with Me scatters abroad"* (NIV). It says we cannot serve two masters. Either we are going to live our lives God's way, or we are not going to do it God's way. The choice is ours. You must run your farm or your business according to God's principles. You cannot have your foot in two camps. Farmers know that sitting on the fence is the most uncomfortable place to be, especially a barbed wire one. An army general always encouraged young Christian soldiers to nail their colours to the mast on the very first night that they slept in their barracks, *"When it's lights out, I challenge them to get on their knees in front of all the other sixty-odd soldiers and make a public confession of their faith. The rest of the soldiers might not like them, but eventually they will be respected."*

Paul's letter to the church in Ephesus is one of my favourite passages. He writes in chapter 3:14–21, *"For this reason, I kneel before the Father, from whom every family in heaven and earth derives its name. I pray that out of His glorious riches he may strengthen you with power through*

His Spirit in your inner being, so that Christ may dwell in your hearts through faith. And I pray that you, being rooted and established in love, may have power, together with all the Lord's Holy People, to grasp how wide and long and high and deep is the love of Christ, and to know this love that surpasses knowledge … that you may be filled to the measure of all the fullness of God. Now to Him who is able to do immeasurably more than all we ask or imagine, according to His power that is at work within us, to him be glory in the church and in Christ Jesus throughout all generations, for ever and ever" (NIV).

It would be remiss of me if I didn't share Billy Graham's prayer of repentance here:

"Dear Lord Jesus, I know that I am a sinner, and I ask for your forgiveness. I believe You died for my sins and rose from the dead. I turn from my sins and invite You to come into my heart and life. I want to trust and follow You as my Lord and Saviour. Amen". This may be prayed as an act of re-commitment, for those who are already believers in the faith. It is a free gift that you cannot afford to refuse. It's a very simple decision which will change your whole life." [39]

Howard Hughes was once one of the most powerful men in the United States of America, but he was known as a recluse. He held the world record for flying around the world in an aeroplane. He was a man who had done everything and been everywhere, yet he eventually lived in total obscurity. A handsome looking man, who weighed something like sixteen stone (104 kg), he was married to a succession of famous film stars, yet he died weighing less than 8 stone (47kg). He was a man totally discontented with life.

In stark contrast to Howard Hughes, the apostle Paul wrote to the Philippians 4:11 (NKJV) *"Not that I speak in regard to need, for I have learned in whatever state I am, to be content."* He had learnt the secret

---

[39] Sinners Prayer taken from Billy Graham Christian Woman Daily Devotional.

of contentment, In Proverbs 30 :9 we read, *Keep falsehood and lies far from me; give me neither poverty nor riches, give me only my daily bread.'* That is a good prayer.

It is time to stop complaining and thank God for what we have. Let us be content with our lives and stop comparing our lot to others.

I am going back to the cottage where Norman was born and where we started our married life. If you compare it with some of the palatial homes around the north coast of Northern Ireland, I would probably be regarded as poor. However, if you compare it with some of the mud and wattle huts I visited in rural Uganda, then I would be regarded as extremely wealthy. True wealth is what we carry inside, peace, love and the greatest treasure - Jesus Christ.

So my friend, be content with what God has given you, and most of all, be thankful, if you are a believer, that your name is written in the Lamb's Book of Life. Be thankful that you know Jesus Christ as your Lord and Saviour, for, *"What shall it profit a man if he shall gain the whole world and lose his own soul?"* (Mark 8:36) KJV.

Photo Memories

Age 10 with my pigtails

Me at age 19

Our wedding day in 1968.

Diana with her supreme champion in the Jersey cattle class.

Mary Ranken Maternity Hospital, Coleraine,
where our children were born.

Our sons and daughter: Ian (5), David (8), Ross (3) and Ruth (1)

Ian, Ross, David and Ruth (2018)

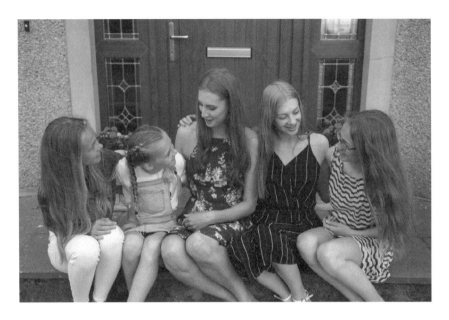

My beautiful girls (grandchildren): Ruby, Isla, Grace, Emma and Hannah

Boy will be boys (grandchildren): Noah, Jamie, Lewis and Sam

Raising money for the Torch Trust for the blind.

Palace of Holyrood House, Edinburgh, my son David and me.

One of the last times we were all together as a family.

For more information visit:
www.Diana McClelland.com

INSPIRED TO WRITE A BOOK?

Contact

Maurice Wylie Media

Your Inspirational & Christian Book Publisher

Based in Northern Ireland and distributing around the world.

www.MauriceWylieMedia.com

Endnote

The Rev T.H. Mullin, B,A,B.D., of Convoy was born in Limavady, the second son of Mr John Mullin, a teacher and farmer. Educated at Main St school, Limavady Academy, Foyle College and Queen's University, he took his Theological course at the Assembly's College in Belfast. He was ordained in Convoy, County Donegal on March 17, 1938, and married Miss Julia Forsythe, B.A., also from Limavady. At the time of the installation at Ballyrashane on a very hot day in July 1948, and at the evening social many men in the gallery had to remove their jackets and sit in their shirt sleeves. There were no t-shirts in the 40s!

After the close of the war, and when materials became plentiful again, a tremendous surge of repairs and building took place throughout Ulster. Ballyrashane was no exception. In the ten years following the war, the new villages were completed at Drumadraw and Ballybogey. Loughanreagh L.O.L. completed the Earl Morrison Memorial Hall in 1953. The Coronation Social Club, headed by some local young men of zeal and vision, completed a fine recreation hall with billiards and other amusements for the young men of the district. Built by voluntary labour, this hall was proved of great benefit to the locality.

In 1953 a project which had originally planned in pre-war years was completed. In April that year a new county primary school and principal's residence was declared open by Mr D. Hall Christie C.B.E., chairman of the Co. Londonderry Education Committee. The new school had accommodation for 100 children and comprised of three classrooms, a combined dining room and assembly hall and an all-electric kitchen. The site cost £500, the school itself cost £16,000 and the principal's residence cost £2,000. Since it closure Ballyrashane Creamery have bought the site for an extension to the creamery.

In 1937 Miss Mary (May) Hamill of Mountsandel, a member of Ballyrashane church, went out as a missionary to Manchuria. Miss Hamill's family had been for many generations connected to the congregation. Miss Hamill left Manchuria in 1941, and she could not return home to Ireland owing to the war, went as a teacher to Jarvie, Alberta. Here she Married Mr W.D, Lea., and after the war was joined by her sisters Jeanie and Margaret who also married Canadians.

During the 1920s the church was enhanced in appearance by most generous gifts from the Norris family. A beautiful individual communion service was presented by Mrs W. J. Morris, The Villa, Ballyrashane, in April 1933. Then in 1937 two magnificent memorial windows were placed, one on either side if the pulpit by Miss Martha S. Norris. These windows which transformed the pulpit end of the church, represent the story of Ruth and Naomi in the Old Testament and the parable of the Good Samaritan from the New Testament. Following the erection of the new church hall in 1986 which adjoins the front end of the church, the lovely memorials have been retained in their original position and illuminated and enhanced by artificial lighting. Miss Norris also acted as honorary organist for many years prior her marriage to Mr A. Forgie.

Dr Mullin was a faithful pastor to the Ballyrashane people and was revered by all who knew him. His qualities as a Church Historian were recognised when the General Assembly conferred on him the degree of Dr of Divinity. He faithfully served his Saviour in Ballyrashane for over 30 years until his retirement.